Temple Israel Library
2324 Emerson Avenue South
Minneapolis, MN. 55405

Please sign your name and telephone number
on the above card.

Books and materials are loaned for a period of
three weeks and may be returned to the Library
or Temple reception desk.

Fines will be charged for any damage or loss of
materials.

DEMCO

The Kosher Pig

And Other Curiosities of Modern Jewish Life

The Kosher Pig

And Other Curiosities of Modern Jewish Life

Richard J. Israel

Alef Design Group

Los Angeles

Library of Congress Cataloging-in-Publication Data

Israel, Richard J.

    The Kosher pig and other curiosities of Modern Jewish life / Richard J. Israel.

      p.   cm.

    ISBN 1-881283-02-x : $18.95

    1. Judaism–United States—Miscellanea.   2. Judaism–20th century.

3. Israel, Richard J.   I. Title

BM205.I82   1993

296' .0973' 09045–dc20   93-2585

                                                      CIP

Published by the Alef Design Group

Alef Design Group

4423 Fruitland Avenue

Los Angeles, California 90058

(213) 582-1200

MANUFACTURED IN THE UNITED STATES OF AMERICA

To:

Alisa

Anna

David

Harold

Joshua

Rachel

Rob

Sam

and those yet to come

My children, their spouses, and my children's children.

כֵּן יִרְבּוּ!

They are, after all, what the effort is about.

Acknowledgments

I wish to acknowledge with thanks those people who read over and made helpful comments on much of this text before it reached its final form: Richard Sherwin, Jeffrey Summit, Dan Wakefield, my wife Sherry, and most particulurly my son Joshua, who worked very hard to keep my writing lean. There may have been others, but given the length of time these essays have been accumulating, I may have forgotten them. I hope they forgive me.

I am grateful to Arthur Green, from whom I originally heard the story of the kosher pig, though at the time neither of us knew what I would do with it. William Novak was a valued source of encouragement and information from the beginning. This also seems like a good place to say thank you to Sheila Decter who was a good friend at a hard time.

A special word of appreciation also to my publisher, Joel Grishaver for believing in the book. I learned elsewhere that it was a fine *second* book which could be published once I had "marquee value." I am grateful that he was willing to take the risk on a group of essays, "...they are notoriously hard to sell" even without the marquee. I hope that his faith will be justified.

Richard J. Israel
Newton Centre, Massachusetts
June 1993

Table of Contents:

Bees and Jews

Running Torah

Epilogue

Introduction

uring the early sixties, when personal discovery was even more fashionable than it is today, I participated in a training program for those who wanted to run the predecessors of what have come to

be known as growth-groups. It was near the end of the second long and very intense summer the ten of us had spent together. We had been talking about each other and about what was going on in our group from nine in the morning to nine at night, with breaks only for meals, coffee and quick trips to the washroom, six days a week. We had grown very close to one another and yet there was one area in which I always felt separate and different from the other members of the group...that was as a Jew.

The feeling was most acute on Friday nights. The group met that evening, the same as it did every other evening. For the rest of the participants, Friday night was no different from Tuesday night. But Friday night is a special time for my wife and children and me. Food, mood and dress are all upgraded. We would have Shabbat dinner together as a family with the appropriate blessings and songs, and then, because we do not drive on Shabbat, I walked the three miles from the little farm house where we were staying to the conference center. I felt absolutely unable to share this part of my life with the others.

Our group was feeling rather self-congratulatory that Friday evening and people spoke of how wonderful it was that we had become so intimate. I didn't feel intimate at all. There were large pieces of me they knew nothing about. My entire experience as a Jew had never once entered into the discussions. I did not volunteer and they did not ask. There was not so much as a comment about why I was wearing a good white shirt and slacks while they were wearing our usual sloppy uniform of shorts and T-shirts. I was annoyed and this time, I said so.

If we knew so much about each other, why didn't they know it was my Shabbat? Why didn't they know that it was a major imposition for me to arrive at our meetings every Friday night? They were completely unaware of a very significant set of my commitments and it didn't occur to any members of our ostensibly intimate group that such things might be important and even worth discussing. With relief, I was finally able to talk about how I was trying to preserve my own private values in a group in which there was great pressure to reveal and share. They were all part of the great majority, while I was all alone. They were under the illusion that I was an authentic part of the group while in fact, they had no idea how isolated I felt.

Perhaps I was overdoing it. I backed off from my tirade and excused myself and them, commenting that it was probably understandable that such things had not occurred to them. If I cared that much, I could have raised these issues earlier. Nevertheless, they should know that they were occurring to me with increasing clarity and intensity by the minute.

It became very quiet in the group. Then the fellow sitting next to me said, "I don't know if any of you has noticed but my left leg is just a little shorter than the right. I wear special shoes to compensate for it, a slightly thicker sole in one shoe so that I don't walk with a limp. Though I don't think anyone here has paid attention, I have always been painfully self-conscious about it. The rest of you were lucky. Your bodies were whole and symmetrical while I was a secret cripple and because of that, I always felt that I was very different from the rest of you."

The person next to him continued without a pause. "You folks are all from the big cities. I was born and raised on Deer Island, off the coast of Maine. You all are so sophisticated. I am just a country boy and will never be more than that."

Then, the woman to his left shyly noted that though we had never said anything about it, we had all certainly noticed that English was not her native tongue, that she spoke with an accent. We were all *real* Americans. She was the *true* outsider of the group.

One after another, all the members of the group shared their oddness, the extent to which each was more different from all the members of the group than anyone else there. To my astonishment, each of them had a significant and often hidden characteristic that made them feel as different and separate as my Jewishness made me feel.

Over the years, I have come to believe that this group was not unique. I have observed the same phenomenon in every group I have ever been in that felt free enough to talk about the subject. Just about everyone feels less a part of every group than everyone else. Every member is secretly convinced that because of a concealed flaw, he or she is the group's one authentic outcast. And so I have come to believe that though being Jewish is different, it may not be more different than being Polish, or Greek, or rich, or having a limp or coming from a farm in Iowa. The particulars are of course very different, but the inner experience of feeling separate may not be.

The Jew in me rejects this thesis. In my gut, I am certain that we Jews are more unique than anyone else. But it is my current suspicion that a lot of other people think the same thing. We Jews may indeed be absolutely unique, but in that, may be very much like everyone else. What may be most different about Jews is that we seem to have taken a nearly universal experience and raised it to the level of a theology, a theology of particularism. It is this conviction about the universality of uniqueness which gives me the courage to write about a series of peculiarly Jewish issues. I hope that they will stimulate readers to reflect upon their own uniqueness and what it means to bring their cultural baggage to bear upon the special complexities of modern living.

This is a book about modernity and being Jewish, about the ironies that result from trying to appropriate the Jewish tradition while at the same time attempting to live fully in the modern world. There is no great trick to living in a traditional Jewish world; it is a world that is self-contained, internally consistent, suspicious of the outside world, though for its members, it is warm and supportive. There is also no great trick to living as a full participant in modern Western culture. This is the air most of the people around me appear to breathe. It, too, is a rich full world. But my struggle has been to try to do both.

This attempt to balance both worlds has affected a large segment of my life. It has conditioned where I went to school, whom I chose to marry, the size of my family, the way I wanted to raise our children, my professional life, what I read and even the way I spend my leisure time. I have always been curious about a wide range of issues but whatever subject I have looked at has always seemed to turn into an inquiry about how it related to the Jews. Since I am bald and Jewish, why *not* write an article about *Baldness and the Jewish Problem?* I have fought my parochialism, but with no success. When with great effort I finally wrote something that had no Jewish references in it and sent it off to a prestigious literary magazine, they sent it back saying they liked the piece, but that it was too Jewish for them to publish. I gave up. I concluded that I was terminally Jewish and should write about what interested me.

What I want to explore in this book are a number of subjects that have caught my fancy over the years, subjects in which the tension between being a traditional Jew and being a modern American are played out. In the course of writing them down, I began to suspect that instead of being both, I may be neither a traditional Jew nor a modern American.

> There was once a Polish Jew who was unhappy living in Poland and who applied for an exit visa to emigrate to Israel. He went to Israel but concluded that he couldn't adjust, was unhappy there and so he got permission to travel back to Poland. Alas, it didn't work out this time either and so once again, he travelled back to Israel.

When the second trip to Israel didn't work out either, he requested permission to go back to Poland. The exasperated Israeli immigration officer said, "You are not happy in Poland so you travel to Israel. You are not happy in Israel so you travel to Poland. So when are you happy?" The man smiled and said "That's easy. When I am travelling."

So it is with me—and perhaps you.

Richard Israel

Old Issues, New Contexts

The Kosher Pig:

When Jewish Law Doesn't Quite Work

 pious Jew was told by his doctor that he had a rare disease, one that could only be cured by his eating pork. The man was determined to triumph over both his disease and its cure. He would eat pork as prescribed by the

physician, since Jewish law holds that saving a life takes precedence over food prohibitions. Nevertheless, he would not eat an animal that had been cruelly killed in the manner of the local peasants. He bought a pig and took it to the town ritual slaughterer, known as a sho<u>h</u>et, who listened sympathetically to the story. The sho<u>h</u>et got a special knife that would never be used on a kosher animal and ritually slaughtered the beast in accordance with the Jewish tradition.

Then, as is customary, the sho<u>h</u>et examined the animal's lungs. He discovered some questionable blemishes on them, blemishes which in a kosher animal would have cast doubts on whether the animal could be eaten. For obvious reasons, the sho<u>h</u>et was not familiar with pig lungs and felt that he could not take it upon himself to determine how serious the blemishes were. Thus the sho<u>h</u>et and the sick man took the dead pig to the rabbi and asked, "Rabbi, is this pig kosher?" The rabbi looked at the animal's lungs for some time and then declared, "It may be kosher, but it is still a pig."

I am often asked questions regarding Jewish law.

Most of them are rather straight-forward:

- "My father died during Adar II, a leap month in the Jewish calender, but there is only one Adar this year, no leap month. On what date do I light a memorial candle to commemorate the anniversary of his passing? "
- "My roommate used one of my aluminum meat pots to cook vegetable soup, but washed it with his regular non-kosher dishes. May I use the pot?"

These are easy. You light the candle during the only Adar you have this year, and no, you should not use the pot without scouring it and boiling it out if you want to keep your things kosher.

3

Some of the questions I get are the questions of innocents.

- "May I say Kaddish, the traditional memorial prayer, for my cat? Such a sweet cat."

  No. If you want to say something nice about the cat, go ahead, but the Kaddish prayer is a prayer for people to say about God, not cats.

- Or, "I know that one should not eat bread during Passover. What about toast?"

  If you are following the laws of Passover, you may not eat toast. You may have forgotten that toast is a form of bread.

Over the years, I have also been asked a third kind of question by friends and strangers and by colleagues who knew of my interest in such things. They are questions the *Shulḥan Arukh*, the standard code of Jewish law, never even thought about, questions a little like those asked of the rabbi in the story that opened this essay, questions I have come to think of as Kosher Pigs:

- The police have been ticketing the High Holiday drivers who park in the vicinity of the synagogue during the hours they are in services. The congregants who haven't been running out to the parking meters to put in coins want the rabbi to complain to the police department about the tickets. They would like him to tell the police that they are interfering with the Jewish religion since, according to Jewish tradition, they are not allowed to come out during services to put money in the meters. In fact, since it is a holiday, they aren't allowed to use money at all.

  The rabbi, who follows traditional practice, doesn't believe they should have driven to the synagogue on the holiday in the first place. The non-Jewish chief of police, who grew up in an Orthodox Jewish neigh-

borhood, believes the same thing. He thinks that if they are not observant enough to walk to the synagogue on a holy day, they are not too
observant to put money in the meters.

What should the rabbi tell the police chief?

Some of the questions I call kosher pigs are about kosher food,
sort of:

• "Peyote buttons are very bitter. Are they kosher for maror, the bitter
herbs we eat at the Passover meal? It would make the celebration very
special."

• "Lunch time, first day of Passover, I am taking a break from the office
to solicit a big gift from a Jewish client for the Federation of Jewish
Philanthropies. Where is a restaurant which is kosher for Passover so
that I can buy a proper lunch for my prospect?"

*He should be in the synagogue, along with the kosher restaurant owners,
not at work, on the first day of Passover! But since he is not in the synagogue and he is working, is it so bad that he wants to take some time out to
raise money for the Jewish poor? Nevertheless, he is not going to find a
kosher restaurant open on the holiday, at least not in our town.*

• "Rabbi, I just completed a hard fifteen mile run this Yom Kippur
morning. It was a great run but now I am feeling terrible. I know this
is a fast day but doesn't Jewish law say that under these circumstances, when my health is endangered, I am supposed to drink?"

• A part-time commercial fisherman in small town in California keeps
squid in his freezer for what he says are strictly professional reasons,
presumably for bait. Squid, which because they have neither fins nor
scales, as required for a kosher fish, are definitely not kosher. He
wants to know whether these squid affect the kosher status of the
kosher meat that he has imported from a hundred miles away. He has
phoned his rabbi on Saturday morning to ask that question.

The rabbi is definitely miffed. He wants to know if the congregant has any justification in asking the question in the first place; if the fellow is so pious—what is he doing phoning me on Saturday morning? How can such a person be taken seriously?

Forget about the squid. They are no problem as long as they are wrapped up and lying quietly in the freezer. The more interesting question revolves around the other part of the question. Traditional Jews do not use electricity on the Shabbat. The making of fire is prohibited on that day and electricity seems close enough to fire that it too is put off limits, including the use of the phone. But if placing a phone call on the Shabbat disqualifies the fisherman from asking a question of Jewish law, does answering a phone call on the Shabbat disqualify the rabbi from answering a question of Jewish law?

Some kosher pig questions are about sex:

- "I am married, non-Jewish and having an affair with a married Jewish man. Is it against his religion to sleep with me when I am having my period?"

  In most Jewish circles, whether traditional or not, their basic relationship would not be given very high marks. But she is not asking about whether she should be having an affair with him. Her question is more focused. She is correct in her understanding that in traditional practice, a man does not sleep with his wife during her period and not afterwards either, until she has been to the Mikveh, a ritual bath in which she completely immerses herself in water so as to be symbolically pure to re-establish their sexual relationship. In a way, some of these issues are a little like a man who has pushed his wife out the window of their tenth floor apartment and who, when he comes to trial, asks the judge whether he is responsible for paying the dry-cleaning bill on her clothing.

- "Should a Jewish lesbian with a Jewish lover use the Mikveh?"

- "An Orthodox rabbi has just made a serious pass at me. Do you think he will want me to go to the Mikveh before I have an affair with him?"
- "May I, an unmarried Jewish woman living with the same Jewish man for a little over a year, go to the Mikveh? It would add a lot to our relationship."

Sometimes sex and food get combined in unlikely ways.

- "Even though we love each other, he doesn't want me to move in with him unless I agree to keep a kosher home, something I have always refused to do. Rabbi, should I keep kosher?"
- "My family keeps our home strictly kosher for Passover which includes getting rid of all leavening. I have a yeast infection. May I go home for Pesa<u>h</u>?"

  Forget it. Bread yeast is what is prohibited. Enjoy your Passover at home.
- It is the practice of the rabbi of the congregation to wear a yarmulke, a skull cap, when saying the grace after meals but only if the meal is kosher. If the meal is not-kosher, he does not wear a yarmulke. A congregant asks, is it appropriate for her to follow the practice of her rabbi at public events and as a matter of respect wear a yarmulke when he does, or may she make her own determination about when she ought to wear a yarmulke?

  Though not precisely a matter of Jewish law, in traditional circles it is a well established custom for men to wear yarmulkes as a sign of respect during devotional moments, and since every moment ought to be devotional, many will keep their heads covered all the time. Eating is considered a devotional act, one which requires a blessing, so covering one's head at mealtime is a very conventional religious gesture. One is not under obligation to say a blessing on non-kosher food which one ought not be eating in the first place. That is probably what the rabbi has in mind as he takes his hat off and on.

7

In Jewish tradition, a married woman covers her hair in public, for the sake of modesty, but would not wear a man's garment, like a yarmulke. The questioner obviously has a view of the world in which men and women have identical religious obligations and finds that that set of obligations comes into conflict with her rabbi's peculiar eating habits and her attempt to be respectful to him.

She is on her own. I can't help her.

Intermarriage is frequently a factor in these questions:

- "Rabbi, I am marrying an Episcopalian woman, but I want to include the traditional seven blessings of the Jewish wedding in our ceremony. Do they have to be in Hebrew or can I translate them into English?"

- "Does the prohibition against weddings during the period between Passover and Shavuot (The Feast of Weeks), apply to our upcoming intermarriage?"

- "I understand that Ashkenazic Jews and Reconstructionists do not name children after living relatives. Since my wife and I are not familiar with these terms, we think we are probably neither. May we give our baby the same name as a living third cousin even if my wife isn't Jewish."

  Too many issues all at once! The following have to be sorted out; Sephardic Jews (Mediteranians) do name after living relatives. Ashkenazic Jews (central and eastern Europeans) do not. But a third cousin would hardly count for either group. Reconstructionists (a modern Jewish denomination) are about as relevant to the question as Socialists or nudists. They are simply not part of that particular act. Finally, you are holding onto a piece of Jewish folk-tradition that has very little to do with Jewish law and you are married to a non-Jew, which is a very large issue in Jewish law—but you have not asked me about that.

Answer: If you have family members who might be offended, you probably shouldn't do it, but if not, it would not matter.

Here is an even less likely version of the intermarriage question that came to me over the phone:

- "I know Jewish law used to say that you must have a Jewish mother or convert to Judaism to be Jewish. I just read in the newspaper that a big Jewish organization says you are also Jewish if your father is Jewish. I am black. Though I was raised in a black family by a black father, I have recently learned that my biological father was Jewish. I am in love with a fine Christian woman and would like to marry her, but do not want to lose God's blessing as a Jew. Now that I am Jewish, am I permitted to marry her?"

The questioner is referring to the current position of Reform Judaism which states that Jewishness can descend from either parent, as long as the children take positive, public steps to affirm their Jewishness. The leaders of Reform Judaism would consider him Jewish but only if he led an active Jewish life. Though the option to become Jewish is easily available to him, it does not sound as if he is interested in picking up that option. On the other hand, the position implicit in the question is the way that most Reform Jews have popularly understood the subject so that most Reform Jews, though not their rabbis, would consider him Jewish. Orthodox and Conservative Jews would not.

Answer: Congratulations on your wedding. I hope you will be very happy. Insofar as you have God's blessing as a Jew, I feel sure you will not lose it through your marriage.

There is something very reasonable about each of these questions. There is also something bizarre about them. In one sense they are very traditional. They are attempts to apply the classic categories of Jewish law to new situations. The problem is that the questioners either do not know about or have rejected some of the most basic presuppositions of the Jewish legal system. There is something in the premise of their questions that prevents a *halakhic* answer, an answer according to traditional Jewish law, from being given. The puzzle we are left with is: Can the *halakhah* be applied to non-*halakhic* questions or must we rely upon the punch line of the old joke and say that you can't get there from here?

Some of the questions I have just described were beyond me. I tried to be polite and hoped the questioners would go away quietly. Others, I felt, needed to be taken more seriously. My initial response to each of these questions was to try to answer a different question. "Consider changing your framework so that you can start out closer to a *halakhic* question." No luck. These people wanted pieces of *halakhah* that could be appropriated. They were not interested in the whole system.

The traditional Jewish response to that position is that if it isn't the whole system, it isn't anything. To pick and choose is not to observe the *halakhah* at all. There is much to recommend such a response. Even I, who try to resolve such questions about Kosher Pigs, must frequently throw up my hands in exasperation, quite unable to figure out a way even to think about the questions. But there are many people out there asking questions that they feel are questions of Jewish law, or at very least, questions of Jewish propriety. Traditionalists who deal with these people forthrightly will often reject their questions and them. Liberals are not much better equipped if they hold that ultimately we are all autonomous and can make whatever decisions we wish. They often find the debates about nuances in Jewish law irrelevant and prefer to focus on what they view as large scale Jewish concerns, like Jewish ethical responsibilities. Gordian knots generally need to be cut and this process tries to untie them.

But those who believe that Jewish law still has life are attempting to deal with the same kinds of problems that Hillel and Shammai, those great teachers of the Talmud, faced with their classic questioners. Are questions that appear to mock the system to be taken at face value or can they be used to instruct the questioner? The way of Shammai, the tough master, is certainly less ambiguous, less time consuming, and easier to justify: Throw them out on their ears.

Still, people who are trying to use the vocabulary of the tradition, even though they can't do much with the syntax, may be offering us an opportunity to teach them. They will tax our patience and ingenuity. It is to encourage us to work in such a direction that our tradition holds up gentle Hillel, who tried to draw people near, as a model teacher, not Shammai.

I have come to believe that we should try to answer these quasi-*halakhic* questions with quasi-*halakhic* answers. We should make the real *halakhic* issue clear, describe why a traditional *halakhic* answer won't work for their questions, and then functioning out of the questioner's framework, bring to bear whatever Jewish sources seem to help.

- "We are going to dinner at the home of a woman whom we know uses lard in her baking. We don't want to embarrass her by telling her we don't eat pork products. After dessert, may we put milk in our coffee?

  The straight Halakhic answer is probably, yes, you may put milk in your coffee after eating lard. It is true that observant Jews do not eat milk products immediately after meat products, but it is also true that observant Jews do not eat lard and so the laws of milk and meat do not apply to prohibited animals. The Bible did not say that you should not boil a pig in its mothers milk. It was from the verses that said that you should not boil a kid in its mother's milk that the laws concerning milk and meat were derived. Maybe if the lady embarrasses that easily, you should find another friend.

  That at least is the answer I might want to give. The answer that I think I should give, even though it is not correct according to halakhah, might be, "No, you should not put milk in your coffee. If you are willing to eat lard and nevertheless you are still asking such questions, you should be reminded of the restrictions of the system."

- "May an immediate relative serve as witness for an egalitarian wedding contract?"

  The traditional wedding contract does not treat the sexes equally, but rather presumes that it is the man's actions that initiate the marriage. A marriage contract in which both the man and the woman are equal initiators would not be a traditional wedding contract. In the traditional version, immediate relatives are construed as potentially involved parties with vested interests and therefore not valid witnesses.

  One answer to the question: Since the document you have created is not a real wedding contract in any event, you can do what you please about witnesses.

  The answer I prefer would be: Since you have consciously altered the traditional document, it would seem that you are treating your modern version of the wedding contract as real and serious. Otherwise, why would you have bothered? As such, it would be appropriate to follow traditional practice and to have your wedding contract signed only by non-related people who could legitimately be viewed as disinterested witnesses.

- May an unmarried Jewish woman living with a Jewish man go to the Mikveh, as asked above?

  Jewish law makes an innocent presumption, or at least a presumption suited to another age, that a Jewish man would never be willing to sleep with a woman in a state of ritual impurity. Unmarried women are therefore not permitted to go to the Mikveh—as a way to keep them from becoming sexually available. Since the woman in this case has been sleeping with him for over a year, it is obvious that in this situation, the system hasn't worked. If she goes to the Mikveh and finds it spiritually rewarding, perhaps we can hope that the atmosphere of a well-run Mikveh might encourage her at least to consider marriage as a more serious option than she previously had.

If we take such questions and questioners seriously, do we not make the liberties they have already taken with the system more available? I think not. They will take whatever liberties they will, with or without our permission. The real issue is one we must deal with constantly these days. Can they be salvaged or should we let them sink? Though full of fear and trembling, I am committed to salvage operations. Good advice may bring a few of them back to better questions. There are absolutely no guarantees.

In 1983, the National Research Council of the U.S. Agency for International Development published a report of a forest animal from Indonesia called a *babirussa* which was described as a kosher pig, a real one. The Council thought that "cultures that do not eat swine might accept the *babirussa*." The *babirussa* was a member of the pig family and was said to have a split hoof and chew its cud. It made the front page of major newspapers throughout the country. How that happened is unclear for the animal had been known about for a long time. Unfortunately, it turned out that it didn't really chew its cud, wasn't kosher and its fifteen minutes of fame were over. That is the danger with kosher pigs, that they often turn out to be more pig than kosher— but they are always worth checking out.

In any event, I love the questions. If you have been asked about any Kosher Pigs lately, please let me know about them.

The Late Jewish People

Shemaryahu Levin, the Zionist teacher and orator, once said that he spent his entire life trying to come late to a Jewish meeting without succeeding. He clearly believed the widely held view that there is such a thing as Jewish

Standard Time. It is my conviction that the notion of Jewish Standard Time is essentially a canard. It is not that Jewish events universally start when they are announced. They don't. The point is, that neither do anyone else's. Well, almost anyone: The Germanic decedents of the Angles and the Saxons and occasional eccentrics among widely scattered ethnic groups do, and that tends to intimidate the rest of us.

And even the Germans are not always punctilious about clock time, at least not if they are German Jews. That fact used to exasperate Leo Baeck, the distinguished rabbi of the Berlin Jewish community, who told me an attempt he made to re-set Jewish time to clock time. As I remember the story, he recounted how he arrived promptly, as always, to a meeting of the Berlin B'nai B'rith lodge of which he was president. Only he and the treasurer of the lodge were present at the time formally designated for beginning the meeting. Annoyed with the lateness of the rest of the members who were supposed to be prompt Germans, and having a pet project that he wanted to support, Baeck proposed that the lodge fund the publication of the revised edition of the Buber/Rosensweig translation of the Bible. The treasurer assented. They wrote the check, funded the translation and adjourned the meeting. Baeck reported that two good things came of that brief meeting: a magnificent Bible translation was published, and no one ever came late to a lodge meeting again.

Rabbi Baeck may have done an admirable thing, but it is somewhat terrifying to contemplate what Jewish life would be like if all the prompt people took such radical steps while waiting for the others to arrive. Everyone else's lives would be thrown into pandemonium. Under the current system, the only issue for the rest of us is to be sure that our general measure of lateness is set to the same standard. If everyone arrives at the same late time, or if people expect you to arrive when you do, you are not late, irrespective of the time that has been announced. The problem is that we now live in a pluralistic society and we have no shared standard of lateness.

If you have candid informants, you can learn about how people view their own group's time sense. I am told that Black people, when speaking among themselves, may refer to Colored People's Time (also known as C.P. Time), and in some circles even talk about Old Colored People's Time (i.e. African Time, which is a bit later than ordinary Colored People's Time). Italian Time, Polish Time, along with a whole host of other ethnic times, are measures of the interval between when an event is announced and when people are actually expected to appear. Unhappily, each ethnic time must be factored differently.

It is not quite clear to me whether my wife's and my families come from different ethnic time zones or if her family just overdosed on the Scandinavian Midwest during the many years they lived there. (The Swedes, like the Germans, follow clock time.) I get very fidgety when I arrive at an airplane more than a minute or two before the plane door closes. I am frequently rewarded for my arrival time by being forced to sit in first class, since my tourist seat has been given away. My wife, on the other hand, is a nervous wreck if we don't get to sit in the waiting room for at least twenty minutes before the plane starts to board. I am always surprised when people actually come at precisely the time they have been invited. I find it a great effort to be ready at clock time. My wife used to be ready early, but there are signs that I may be succeeding in adjusting her time standard. "Temporal Intermarriages" have to bear a heavy burden. If one of the parties is forever on German time while the other is on Polish time, they both feel put upon with great frequency.

Woody Allen describes a planet in another galaxy where the civilization is more advanced than ours by fifteen minutes. That extra fifteen minutes prevents people from having to rush to get to appointments on time. A standardized margin of free time would be a great boon to us all, because if you don't know your guest's or your host's ethnic time factor, you can cause one another a great deal of embarrassment. It is possible to stay up all night in sweaty anxiety to be sure you will arrive precisely at clock time for a very important appointment, only to discover that the person you are to meet doesn't keep clock time.

But intercultural time conflicts can occasionally bring out the best in us. One of my most treasured family memories, an incident which caused me to be extraordinarily proud of my wife and children, happened because we did not know enough about Russian time. My wife and I had met a refusenik mathematician in Leningrad, a charming man who had been trying to get out of Russia for a long time. When we returned to Boston, we went on the circuit for a while and gave slide-lectures about the Jewish families with whom we had visited. We included pictures of our friend Mischa.

At one lecture, someone in the audience said, "He isn't in Leningrad, he is in Boston." Mischa didn't have our address and couldn't have found us. We were surprised and delighted with the news and immediately tracked him down. Would he and his family please come and join us for a Shabbat dinner? We would sit down to eat at 6:00. Both he and we were delighted with the prospect. At the time, our four children ranged in age from seven to thirteen. They had heard how we had met Mischa and were very excited at the prospect of meeting him as well. When seven o'clock arrived and Mischa had not come, we could no longer prevent our children from falling apart. We sat down to eat, having given up on our guests.

We finished dinner and cleared the table. An hour and forty five minutes after our announced time, Mischa and his family arrived. At first we expected some kind of explanation or apology, but then we noticed that they showed no signs of realizing that anything was amiss. My wife and I exchanged glances. We guessed at the nature of our miscalculation. She re-set the table without saying a word. The rest of us chatted informally in the living room. When everything was back in place, we invited the children and they came to the table without a hint about the peculiarities of the situation. Even though they were young, they had learned far more about the responsibilities of hosts than I had ever suspected.

We had a lovely Shabbat dinner together. The only tense moment of the evening came when Mischa commented about how curious it was that our robust looking children had such modest appetites. We smiled a little at one another but we never told him. Someday, someone may encourage Mischa to adjust his lateness standard but it wasn't going to be we that Shabbat evening.

Speed Davening

Sometimes, I pretend that if I were given those three wishes you get in fairy tales, I would use up one of them to check out other peoples' silent prayers. Are they really able to *daven* as fast as they seem to? Once, at Reb Arele's synagogue in

Jerusalem, I got ahead of all the other daveners*. I was surprised, because that was the only time that ever happened to me anywhere. I am a middle-speed davener. I usually do my best to rush along at what is for me a break-neck *davening* speed, only to discover that I am still behind everyone else. I had not realized that slow *davening* was one of the specialties of Reb Arele's ḥasidim.

The traditional Jewish service has a very complex structure. In addition to what we customarily think of as prayers, it contains details about animal sacrifices, rules for interpreting Biblical texts, songs, confessionals, medieval poems about God and a lot more. Over the years, just about everything it started out with has been added to. The service has gotten rather long.

There are several ways of dealing with long. Liberals cut chunks out of the service. The traditionalists don't think much of that procedure. Rabbi Abraham Isaac Kook was traveling through Russia and spent the night at the inn of an isolated little village. In the morning, after prayers, he noticed the Jewish inn-keeper tear off a page from his big prayerbook, roll it up into a tube, put the end in the fire and then use it to light his pipe. When the inn-keeper realized that Rabbi Kook was visibly upset at what he had done, the inn-keeper reassured him. "Don't worry," he said. "I have been doing this for years and I am nowhere near any of the essential prayers." But Rabbi Kook and we know perfectly well that no matter how thick his prayerbook is, sooner or later, the essential prayers are going to go up in smoke. That concern has kept traditionalists from being willing to cut.

Daven, pronounced *dah-ven*, is a Yiddish term which refers, in a comfortable way, to saying prayers. It is of obscure origin. Some say it comes from the same Latin root that produces the English word "Divine," while other derive it from the German or Persian. Its non-Jewish origins have have long since become irrelevent and it is now about as Jewish a word as one can imagine. It has no direct Hebrew or English equivalent. As used in this essay, *Daven* will be treated as a classic "*Yinglish*" word in which the Yiddish root is given English endings.

So what can you do if the service is long, indeed, very close to the maximum attention span of even rather pious Jews, and you are committed to leaving the text intact or maybe even adding a few little things but still have to get to work on time during the week and home for a Shabbat lunch by noon? One conventional solution is to go very fast. To promote "fast" training, more than one Jewish school offers little gold stars to the students who are the quickest through their prayers. But, even when we call it synagogue skills training, we are a little embarrassed about the practice.

A number of years ago, I was escorting a group of American college students through *Hechal Shlomo,* the seat of the Israeli Chief Rabbinate. We passed one room which was marked "Rabbinic Court." To many American Jews, who only see their rabbis preaching and conducting services, the notion that Jews have a functioning Jewish legal system is rather odd. "Why should rabbis need a court?" one of the students asked our rabbinic guide. "Well," he said with a twinkle, "this is where we give out tickets for speeding through the eighteen Amidah prayers."

I don't think he meant it, though. Outside of the *Yeshivot* and a few very special places like Reb Arele's, most of the Jews I know who *daven,* *daven* fast. A friend tells me that when he asked a Lubovitcher Ḥasid he knows, why he davened so fast, the Lubavitcher responded, "So that Satan can't catch me." The implication was that if you *daven* fast enough, you can avoid distractions. If you slow down, and have a short attention span like most of us, you can get into trouble. There is a case to be made for fast praying.

Herbert Benson, author of *The Relaxation Response,* attempted to find out if Transcendental Mediation really did something that could be measured. It did. It lowered the heart rate and blood pressures of its practitioners. But Dr. Benson recounts that he also used an Orthodox morning worship group as one of his control groups and discovered that traditional *davening* did exactly the same things to the heart rate and blood pressure that T.M. did... as long as you didn't concentrate on the words. If you slow down and think about the words, *davening* may do good things for your religious attitude, but it won't do much for your heart and blood pressure.

Prayer has far more to do with feelings and emotions than it does with intellect. What individual words mean counts for much less than what all the words mean together. "Prayer is a right brain activity," as Harold Kushner has written. One of the real problems presented by praying in up-to-date English is that concentrating on the meaning interrupts the flow of the heart. It is only when we don't hear the English any more because we know it so well that we are able to *daven* again.

We really should have known that all along, because it is perfectly clear to all of us that many of our grand or great grand-parents expressed a lot more religious passion in quickly going through prayers they didn't understand than we do fussing over each word to see that it articulates all of our current convictions with precision. Praying fast does work for many people.

But you have to be a regular davener to be a fast *davener*. Once you have so mastered the prayers that they come automatically, individual ideas jump out at you from the prayerbook when you need them. Routine *davening* is necessary if you are to cultivate the special. But while speed *davening* may be fine for the regulars, less experienced daveners need to go more slowly and more carefully. A casual Sunday afternoon driver tying to keep up at the Indy 500 would have some real problems. The same thing can happen to new daveners who try to keep up with the crowd.

I was working at the office in the Hillel Foundation, late on a Sunday afternoon in the summer. It was one of my favorite times to work because the building was usually empty and I could concentrate on hard projects. All of a sudden I heard a blood-curdling scream. Not just an eek-I-have-seen-a-mouse shriek, but a deep throated, terror filled shriek.

From my desk drawer I picked up the old Arab knife that I use as a letter opener and went running from my office, through the building lounge and on to the entrance and stairwell to the upper floors. I didn't know what I would find or what I would do if I did find some terrible thing. When I arrived at the foot of the stairs I realized that the place was again just as quiet as it had been before the scream. There was no blood, no body, and as near as I could tell, there were only two other people in the building, the student I saw *davening* his afternoon prayers in the corner as I went tearing through the lounge, and the janitor who was probably in his apartment in the basement.

As I hurried back to my office through the lounge I saw the janitor walking toward me. "Herb," I said, "Did you hear that terrible scream?"

"Yup." he said, with no emotion.

"What happened?" I asked, still trying to catch my breath.

He shifted his eyes toward the *davening* student. "I don't know much about your Jewish religion," Herb said, "but that kid in the corner..." and he nodded toward the student.

I turned to the student. I was not very successful in concealing my alarm. "Is anything wrong? Can I help in any way?"

"Just leave me alone." he said angrily. Then he picked up his guitar and book bag and marched out of the building.

When I collected my wits I phoned one of the other staff members. "Do you know what just happened?" Then I nervously told my story.

"Oh, that," said my colleague indulgently, "that's just Jimmy the Screamer."

"Jimmy the Screamer?"

"Sure. He has been having some real trouble keeping up with the cantor during the prayers. The cantor always gets ahead of him at services and the poor kid gets upset. He was quiet about it until he took a course in primal screaming. Then he began to get a little noisy during services, so we suggested he come practice *davening* here when the building wasn't busy.

"Some of the time, when he slows down he thinks about the cantor getting ahead of him and he gets rattled, but then settles himself down with a good scream or two. Don't worry about a thing. He is just fine. He's a great screamer, isn't he?"

So if you haven't *davened* for a long time and don't *daven* regularly, don't try to *daven* fast no matter how easy the pros make it seem. If you do, it could turn out that fast *davening* will do very little either for your spiritual life or your blood pressure. It certainly didn't do much for mine that day. I just went home and poured myself a stiff drink.

Why tell this story? To explain, I shall have to tell a story.

A number of years ago, a Baptist minister was praying over pea plants and urging the Lord to make the pea plants he was praying for bigger and stronger than the ones he wasn't praying for. And as a testimony to the power of prayer, he reported that that was exactly what did happen.

Zalman, a friend of mine who is a trifle eccentric in these matters decided that if Baptist prayers worked and the experiment was real, Jewish prayers should work too. He was at a Jewish summer camp where he replicated the experiment by planting two rows of beans. He asked a camper to select one of the rows of beans for prayer, to tell no one which it was and then to deposit his choice in the camp safe. A group of campers then prayed twice each day over the plants, but directed their prayers to the unknown row of plants that had been selected.

They watered and weeded both rows all summer and attempted to take care of them equally. At the end of the summer they pulled out the plants, weighed and measured them and sure enough, the beans in one row were significantly larger than the other. But which row were they supposed to be praying for? They asked the camper who had made the choice. He had forgotten. They rushed him to the camp safe to find the slip of paper. They read it and found that the row that had the taller and plumper beans was the row they were not praying for.

My friend, who is really a very pious person in his own special way, then began to reflect on what it all meant. He concluded the following: If the beans in the row they had prayed for had gotten big in response to their prayers, they would have learned that God could be manipulated. If large bean plants had been randomly distributed between both rows, they would have learned that God does not care about prayers. As it turned out, they learned that God does indeed pay attention to prayers, but then feels no compulsion to do what we want.

Prayer is a curious business. There are no results that can be guaranteed in advance, or even in retrospect. We never quite know what will come of our efforts, whether we will lightly touch One who is well beyond our grasp or will merely do a little something for our blood-pressure. We can work very hard to achieve a religious experience and not find it. Sometimes, we do not struggle at all and find one dropped in our laps. Styles of worshiping that work for one person may be of no value for another and even styles that work one day or in one prayer, don't work for another day or another prayer. The best we can do is initiate prayer in our bumbling incompetent ways and, like the illiterate little boy in the Hasidic story who offers God the letters of the alphabet, hope that the One who is the Source of all words, will rearrange them in the way that seems best.

Torah and Telephones

ike many of the <u>H</u>asidic masters, Rabbi Avraham Yaakov of Sadagora was fascinated by the developing technology of his time. He believed that Torah could be seen in all of the new devices that affected nineteenth century life. He taught that from a train, one could learn that because of one second, a person can miss everything. From a telegraph, that every word is counted and charged. From the telephone, that what we say here is heard there. He was looking for Torah in the right place.

These days, the place we especially need to work at finding Torah is in our technology-filled daily lives. My current passion is the Torah of the telephone. Because it has become such a conventional device, we forgot how important it is to ground its use in Jewish values.

A young woman came into my office. She was crying. Her boyfriend had just been seriously hurt in an automobile accident. Did we have a chapel in which she could pray? Of course we did. I took her upstairs. It was summertime, hot and humid. Everything had swelled. The door was stuck and there was nothing I could do to get it open. No matter. I would call a nearby synagogue. There would be no problem.

The first synagogue I phoned made its position clear right away. Strangers weren't permitted to pray there. Besides, she might be crazy.

The second synagogue's secretary asked me if I knew how much it would cost to turn on the light in its large sanctuary.

The third synagogue's secretary said that mid-week, during the summertime, the synagogue was closed altogether. Even a *member* wouldn't be allowed in. I phoned the downtown synagogue association office, which has a chapel, and told them how exasperated I was. The secretary, who thought she was being helpful, suggested that since the men had already finished the afternoon's *minhah* service, the woman could come down the next day for *minhah* and could stand in back. She felt sure the men wouldn't mind too much.

By this time, I was angry. I indicated in a very firm tone that the woman was coming down at that moment and they would have to figure out a way to solve the problem. Well, said the secretary somewhat nervously, she guessed she could get the chapel opened and have the janitor stand there with the young lady as long as she wanted to pray. Outrageous! It is true that Jews generally don't make requests like this. More's the pity, but shouldn't they be helped when they do? (Mind you, all of this happened before the current rash of Torah thefts.)

The next day I wrote a letter in multiple copies about the incident to every one of the rabbis whose synagogues were involved. A few days later I got a note from every one of them, saying that they had checked the matter out with their secretaries and there must have been some mistake. They had been assured that no such calls ever came in. It must have been while the regular secretary was out to lunch, or maybe someone misunderstood the message. Without wanting to belabor the matter, I could tell an almost identical story about the time I tried to get free tickets for the High Holiday services for newly-immigrated Russian Jews and got nowhere with the secretaries. Those rabbis too were certain that such a thing could never have happened in their synagogues.

In my own shop, a Hillel director had told his secretary that he had to prepare for class and did not wish to be disturbed. A call came in to report that a student had just committed suicide and they needed the rabbi at once. She was very sorry, but the rabbi couldn't be disturbed. I was glad that I was there to tell her to pick up the phone and call him that minute. I shudder to think of other calls he may never have gotten, when I wasn't there to make a fuss.

Since many of its clients were Russians, a Jewish agency I know hired a group of Russian women to answer the phone. In theory, it was a wonderful idea serving several needs., but because the women were never adequately trained and because the culturally inherited style of the Russian office bureaucrat is often less than friendly, phoning this agency was *only* for the hardy. The Russian clients may have found the telephone style comfortingly familiar, but everyone else I heard from experienced it as extraordinarily intimidating.

Unwittingly, many of us with responsibilities for the management of Jewish organizations have trained our staff people to believe that their primary function is to protect the institutions and the executives they are working for instead of protecting values of the tradition that both should be serving. Though they are good and honorable people, they need to understand that in the long run, if they view themselves only as advocates of their institutions or their bosses, they will not be effective advocates for either. The first person reached in any agency is usually the phone answerer. That person should be viewed as a professional outreach worker who should be carefully schooled for responsibility.

This means that people who phone us should be made to feel that we are glad they called. If there is a *halakhah* of the telephone, I am sure it includes the passage from *Pirke Avot* that says, "Greet everyone cheerfully." People should be encouraged to believe that we would much rather say yes to a request than no, that we are in business to be of help to them, not to guard ourselves. Those who call should be given information they seek or told where we think they can get it. They must not be lectured at for their foolishness, even if we think they are foolish.

Experience has taught me that whenever I have lost patience and chastised callers, I have only made them angry, not wise.

People may not be put on hold for long periods of time, even if the telephone plays music at them while they wait. They should not be asked who they are before being told whether the person they are seeking is in. If you can't speak with everyone who phones, there are better responses than telling people you are not there if you are. "X is in, but I don't know if she can speak with you just now. Who is calling?" is certainly a preferable response.

It is an act of wanton irresponsibility for an agency executive to ignore both the style and substance of the people who answer office telephones. The calls that come in are both trivial and profoundly serious, wrong numbers and requests for help that are exquisitely embarrassing to the asker. The person most strategically located to welcome or turn away the tentative, the fragile or the marginally attached Jew is the person who answers the telephone.

If the ultimate object of our work is to save the Jewish people or provide Jews with access to the eternal values of our tradition, then we have got to persuade the gatekeepers to those values that they are engaged in a holy task. Remember, it is very hard to know when Elijah has come to visit. He almost always wears ingenious disguises. It is even harder to know when he is on the other end of the telephone line. We have all got to be *very* careful.

Some Jewish Life Skills

How to Survive your Synagogue

S ome Jews don't belong in synagogues. I actually know a lovely man who fainted every time he went inside one. On the other hand, some Jews are quite pleased with things just as they are. They see the synagogue as a place of community. In it they experience friendship, support, and the good feeling that comes from worshiping in a style that feels right. But there is a third group that finds it as difficult to live with the synagogue as as to live without it. It is for them that this chapter is written.

They are people who are looking for a place to make important Jewish religious discoveries. Sometimes they are vaguely dissatisfied with some or all of the following: the style of the service, the rabbi, the other congregants, the decorum, the lack of decorum, the liturgy, the amount of Hebrew, the role of women in the service, the ideology.

If this list includes you, you may have some vague longings for something different. You probably want to glow a little when you leave the synagogue. You want to be gently moved by something you don't quite understand but know is very powerful. You want to feel that there is life in Torah. You may be flirting with Jewish observance, but it doesn't quite make sense to you yet. Or it makes a little sense, but you would like it to make a lot more sense for all the trouble it causes you. You need the synagogue to help you along, but how are you going to grow spiritually in a synagogue full of good people with slightly shriveled souls who seem to love responsive readings?

The truth is that it can be hard to make serious Jewish religious discoveries in many synagogues today. Joseph Campbell takes an even harder line when he says that the function of organized religion is to *keep* people from having religious experiences. I can't go that far, yet it is true that most of the regulars in the synagogue near where you live have settled into comfortable patterns of behavior. They are married people looking for areas of stability in a too-complicated world. They want the relationships between themselves to be relatively predictable. That is not an evil wish. It only means that your average synagogue goers are not likely to be engaged in the Grand Quest.

They are not searching for what is Absolutely True, at least not any more. Maybe they did once, but by now they have either decided that they are not ever going to get answers to big questions, which they have accordingly stopped asking, or (more probably) they have forgotten what the questions were. Now they are doing something else, something equally hard or maybe even harder. They are trying to raise children, make a living, keep up with the mortgage payments, and somehow remain reliable committed members of the Jewish community. They are much more heavily devoted to concreteness than to spirituality. It is a good thing for all of us that they are there, for without them there wouldn't be a synagogue for the religious adventurers to want to improve.

If you are one of the searchers, your rabbi is probably puzzled by what to do about your needs and probably wants the same things that you do for the synagogue. Your rabbi wants Jews to be more Jewishly learned, more committed to the rhythms of the Jewish year, more faithful in their participation in the life of the synagogue, more devoted to Israel and to righting the injustices of society. But the members of the congregation are very far from these goals and here you are, pushing for spiritual values and even asking to institutionalize this interest. What you are talking about seems so remote and messianic that it is hard to take seriously.

If you are only an occasional attender who expects the synagogue to launch your prayers heavenward, then forgive me but I have to give you a brief lecture. It is reasonable to want the synagogue to provide you with an environment in which true prayer is possible. It is not reasonable to expect the synagogue to provide you with a spiritual iron lung, to do for you what you cannot do for yourself. The essential work must be done by you. All that you can hope the synagogue will do is give you a small boost, help you along, provide you with a few people who are trying to accomplish what you are.

You couldn't swim the English Channel as a three-times-a-year swimmer, and you are not very likely to get high in the synagogue if you only appear there three times a year. But what if you are a serious religious searcher who has tried often and long; what if you are not just a passing *kvetch*? How then can the synagogue help you find what you are looking for?

First of all, you have got to understand the acoustic principles of synagogues. Formal synagogues are very quiet, usually too quiet for my taste, but less formal synagogues, which are usually the more traditional ones, are zoned for sound. Knowing that, you should locate yourself to suit your mood.

People who want to talk sit in the back rows. People who really want to *daven* sit forward. If you sit very far back you will probably only hear talk about the stock market or the ball games. Midway along you may pick up some comments about the sermon or hear a discussion of an issue raised by the Torah reading. But if you really want to worship in a serious way, then go forward as far as you dare, hoping that you will not be too conspicuous.

Some of the larger congregations are plagued with really tough ushers who are made extraordinarily anxious by any change from the usual. They believe they know what you ought to do and where you ought to sit. Take heart. After they get to know you, a brief conversation before services may help get you a bit more freedom than is normally accorded the Bar Mitzvah crowd—and the Bar Mitzvah crowd really is in danger of running amok unless governed with a firm hand.

Getting some private space in which to *daven* is much easier if you are a male and your synagogue is one in which a large tallit can be worn without giving an usher a heart attack. With your head covered by a large tallit, you can have all the aloneness you need right there in the presence of a community of Jews. And if the buzz of *davening* in your vicinity is right, you may really be able to pray. It is in the tension between privacy and community that Jewish prayer is located.

A note of caution, however: if you sit there wrapped up in a big tallit and if that is not the convention of your synagogue, people are going to assume that you are super-pious, and you are going to have to learn to live with those assumptions. A compromise is to hide in your tallit only on special occasions, like Yom Kippur. That will be less peculiar; besides, that is a time when, given the crowds, you will need your privacy a lot more and be noticed a lot less.

Because the tallit is useful in helping men to pray, some women have taken to wearing them as well. But that occasionally provokes so much reaction that in your self-consciousness you can get about as much *davening* done as if you were sitting there naked. Some women have tried to wear a shawl instead, the more adventurous, a shawl with fringes. But male or female, you are not going to be able to worship successfully in a tallit or its equivalent until you are able to do so unselfconsciously.

Perhaps you should try wearing it at home first, for practice. If your synagogue is altogether the wrong setting for a tallit, try closing your eyes. Also consider sitting in the unused chapel for part of the service. The variation in congregational attitudes to such matters is enormous. You will undoubtedly have a sense of what to expect in yours.

One of the characteristics of many synagogues is that the worship moves along rapidly. Just when you want to dive in and really work through an issue that the prayer book has suggested, the congregation is already moving on. Don't be intimidated. If you aren't ready to move on, don't. Stay as long as you need to, whenever you wish. Try limiting yourself to a verse or two and really work at them in order to rediscover life in words that have died. You may want to stand and sit with the rest of the congregation, at least if people do those things all at the same time in your synagogue, but don't be hurried through the text unless you are comfortable doing so (See *Speed Davening*).

As a matter of fact, you can decide beforehand that you are not even going to try to keep up, that it is going to take you six months to go through the entire service, and that you are not going through more than two or three prayers on any given week. You may find that you want to join in with the congregation on some of the more familiar refrains, but you don't need to decide about that until you see how it feels. Humming to yourself melodies of your choice can add much to your *davening*. However, doing this while the congregation sings another melody is next to impossible.

Much of the prayerbook was committed to writing only to help the people who couldn't manage to formulate their own prayers. Use it as a springboard, not an anchor. If you can function well on your own, you do not need to be limited to the text.

At the same time, recognize that the traditional siddur contains a lot more than just prayers in the ordinary sense of the word. It is a veritable liturgical anthology. You can learn from it, fight with it, be infuriated by it. It is variously meditative, didactic, polemical, philosophical, poetic, historical; but whatever it is, it is always exceedingly busy. It can argue with you, offer consolation, raise questions, and offer answers It has a lot of material that can keep you going if the creativity of your own head or soul has dried up.

There are other solutions to the problem of what to do when you seem to dry up inside; if there is too much sermonizing that doesn't help you; or, worse yet, if the service or sermon makes you angry. There is literature that you can appropriately read in a synagogue setting. One of the more obvious choices is the Torah text that the synagogue provides. It, and its notes, are chock-full of information, pieties, neat little sermons, and, most important, the text of the Torah. Most synagogues will have one immediately available for you, but even if yours doesn't, having one with you is not likely to upset the people who are sitting near you. You shouldn't have to be a Marrano, but once again the problem is that if they get too upset, you are going to have difficulty concentrating.

There are other books that are serviceable in this context as well. High on the list should be the Hertz prayer book, because of its rich content. It has another advantage; it has both a Hebrew and an English text. If you are sitting with a Hebrew book in your hands, whoever is sitting next to you will conclude that you can't be all bad. When you become more daring, you can bring texts without any Hebrew.

This is easier to do on the High Holidays, when you will be in the synagogue for a long time at a stretch. Then, whoever is sitting near you will soon be reconciled to sitting near a friendly alien and will be borrowing your books in no time. I recommend texts like:

Hammer on the Rock: A Midrash Reader, edited by Nahum Glatzer (New York: Schocken, 1957).

Tales of the Ḥasidim, collected by Martin Buber (New York: Schocken, 1947).

And for the High Holidays in particular consider:

Days of Awe, by S. Y. Agnon (New York: Schocken, 1959).

Justice and Mercy, by Max Arzt (New York: Holt, Rinehart, 1963) a commentary on the traditional liturgy.

The Rosh Hashanah Anthology and *The Yom Kippur Anthology* by Philip Goodman (Jewish Publication Society, 1970 and 1971).

Once you begin to see what works for you, a few hours of browsing in your local Jewish bookstore may provide you with a lot of material. Keep in mind that if you come to synagogue with young children you should certainly provide them with Jewish stories that are appropriate to their age level. Fair is fair.

You should know in advance that you are not going to have the same degree of spiritual earnestness whenever you go to the synagogue. Some of the time, perhaps more often than you think, you will be quite content—maybe even refreshed—just to visit with someone you haven't seen for a while.

Who knows? Once or twice you might even want to talk about the stock market! If that happens, don't be too hard on yourself. You are not a religious failure. You will merely have made an important discovery—that a good synagogue should be designed to absorb many moods. It should have a place for you along with all of your fellow congregants at your best and at your most trivial as well. Just hope that you don't have to feel guilty for having been too judgmental when you were feeling high-minded. Relax, sit in the back row, and have a good Shabbat shmoose with a friend. Maybe you'll be back in the front row next week.

As a final piece of advice, consider trying to find a subgroup of people with concerns like yours, people who would find congenial the same style of worship that you do. The congregation may even welcome the formation of such an additional minyan, since the idea of a pluralistic synagogue has gained some acceptance lately. It can also be that the idea will meet with congregational resistance. If that happens, you may want to meet with your little subgroup on a once-a-month basis, though it is much harder to develop a successful worship pattern on an irregular basis.

Incidentally, these remarks have been directed primarily to the experiences you are likely to have at Shabbat services. Daily services are likely to provide an easier atmosphere in which to express your own peculiar interests, but since in most synagogues these days they are designed primarily for people who want to say Kaddish, the service moves at what some find to be an absolutely alarming rate. Before you catch your breath, the service may be over. Try it, though. You may be lucky enough to find some good daily services.

Try not to stray too far from your synagogue. You need each other more than you may think. There are occasions when one has to break and formally organize something new, but that should only be a last resort. Before you do that, you should be quite convinced that what you are leaving is hopeless and that what you are forming will be better.

How to Give A D'var Torah:

A Beginner's Guide

I am not sure how much can be taught about giving a d'var Torah. Some rabbis who have been at it for years have never learned how. And we all know innocents who just jump in and come up with pearls. Maybe it comes with the genes, but I am going to assume, at least on a provisional basis, that it is possible to teach people something about how to address a holy congregation in such a way that Torah is communicated. You may never become a great Torah teacher, but you don't need to know everything to teach something. Besides, teaching is the best way to learn.

Things to Consider

Your d'var Torah will almost inevitably fall into some rather specific categories or combinations of a couple of them.

The Microscope: From close up you look at very small fragments of a text in great detail and hope that as you magnify the specks you will discover whole worlds within them. You have to be sure to pick up your specks with care, but you will know that you have some nice ones if the commentators are as interested in them as you are. If they aren't, chances are you should forget it too.

Example: Take the first word of Genesis or, better yet, the first word of Leviticus (which you'll need more because the story line is not as interesting), and describe how a series of biblical commentators have treated that word, what problem it represented for them, and what generalizations can be made about their resolutions.

The Airplane: Observe the text from a distance, survey the panorama, take note of interesting details, and then as you descend make observations on why the trip was worthwhile in the first place and how to appropriate that which you have just observed for your more earthbound existence. The Airplane is especially suitable for those Torah readings which deal with ritual details at great length.

Example: After describing the architecture of the *Mishkan* (the Tabernacle), and its role in the lives of people, you might want to discuss the role of minutiae in the building of a religious life. As the French say, God is to be found in the details.

Or: A discussion of the Mishkan often suggests an evaluation of the difference between a Judaism which is fixed in one place, Jerusalem and the Temple, and the portable Judaism of the Mishkan which can be carried about wherever we go.

The Diving Board: This one begins with an idea from the text, takes a big jump and carries it into another issue of greater interest to you.

Example: If the text deals with the furniture of the Mishkan, you can talk about the history of the artifacts used in the synagogue,. Or if the the text devotes a lot of attention to the dress of the priest, you can discuss Jewish traditions about dress and articles of clothing, the significance of the *tallit*, the *kippah*, the special hats Jews were required to wear in the Middle Ages, or the self-imposed restrictions that Jewish communities once placed on fancy clothing.

If the text contains long lists of names, you can present a history of the origins of some characteristic Jewish names, including the names of some of the people who will be present when you speak. If you are new at giving divrei Torah, the thematic approaches represented by the Airplane and the Diving Board may be the easiest for you to handle. Unless you are basing yourself on a traditional commentator, stay away from forms like Microscope or Puzzle (see below) until you know enough Hebrew to be able to distinguish between a real nuance in the text and a mere idiosyncrasy of translation.

The Snuff Box: This is a less respectable version of the Diving Board. A visiting *maggid*, or preacher, used to go from one community to the next. Just before he began his only sermon, his snuff box would drop out of sight. "Where is it?" he would ask loudly. "It has vanished, swallowed up the way the earth swallowed up Korach and his company...which reminds me of an important thought about Korach."

Inventing a non-existent relationship between the text and a talk you would like to give is a technique generated by desperation. If you have just looked at the *parashah* (the weekly Torah reading), for the first time the morning you have to speak and you have discovered that there isn't even any good commentary on the text, then you are in deep trouble and may have to bail yourself out. But even then, the Snuff Box approach is definitely shabby. When you are finished speaking, your listeners have the right to expect that they will know at least some small new thing about the Torah they didn't know before. The Snuff Box rarely provides that. You may be sufficiently stuck that you have no alternative, but this is not a method of which you should be particularly proud.

Occasionally you will have an idea that can legitimately be attached to a number of texts. If, for example, you want to talk about the significance of miracles and have a talk in mind, you can probably hang it on several *parashot* (plural of *parashah*) where miracles are found. Such a d'var Torah should not be considered a Snuff Box.

The Biblical Personality: Dealing with the narrative portions of the Torah, it is possible to analyze the characters of biblical figures and the events of their lives in ways that will shed some light on our own. Some of the standard subjects in this category include Jacob and Esau or Joseph and his brothers and the problems of sibling rivalry and preferred children; or Sarah and Hagar and the jealous wife. Louis Ginzberg's *Legends of the Jews* (Jewish Publication Society) can often be of great assistance in supplementing your sense of a biblical character. Originally published in six volumes, it is also condensed into one thick paperback. *A Certain People of the Book* by Maurice Samuel (Knopf) can also be helpful in this area.

The Puzzle: People love to solve puzzles. If there is classic form for the d'var Torah, this is it. You present several apparently discrepant facts or texts and then explain how the contradictions aren't contradictions at all, but instead point to a deeper meaning that was not obvious at first.

Example: Light was created on the first day of creation, while the sun and the moon were not created until the fourth. Where did the original light come from? Rashi has an answer; in fact, he has several answers. So does contemporary physics. Can one derive an authentic Jewish response to the creationism controversy from these texts?

Or: Why is the story of the mission to find Isaac a wife repeated four times, each time with slight differences?

Or: The Torah tells us that we are not permitted to eat leaven on Passover because the people of Israel did not have enough time to allow their bread to rise as they hurried out of Egypt. But they *did* have leaven in their bread. Why should we not have been told simply to bake our leavened Passover bread quickly before it has time to rise? That would have been a closer approximation to this important incident in our history.

Or: Consider the riddle of the red heifer (Numbers 19) whose ashes are used to purify the people who are impure but which make impure the pure who do the purifying. Attempts to solve this one or just shed some light on it have been the subject of innumerable divrei Torah throughout the ages.

Nehama Leibowitz in her volumes complied as *Studies in the Weekly Sidra* (W.Z.O., Jerusalem) is particularly skillful in the creation and resolution of such puzzles. She never lets her readers off easily, so they still have quite a bit of work to do even after reading her material. But she brings a great deal of interesting rabbinic literature, that is otherwise not available in English, to bear on the questions she considers.

Classical Jewish literature loved the "Puzzle" technique, which in its more elaborate form is known as *pilpul* (literally pepper—i.e. a sharp performance). These days, except in very specialized communities, one has to be careful not to get as carried away by it as our forefathers sometimes were. The number of contradictory facts that a contemporary Jew—even a smart one—can carry is rather limited. Don't build too clever a structure or it will fall apart and you will lose everyone.

The Historian: Historical insights can sometimes open up a text in an exciting way. Even if you don't draw any deep morals, people are frequently delighted and enriched when they see a text in its historical setting.

Example: Verse 1:9 in Song of Songs says, "My love, you are like a mare among Pharaoh's chariots." Buckets of ink have been used to describe the literary significance of that particular image, but Marvin Pope's commentary in the *Anchor Bible* deciphers this verse with ease. In the ancient Middle East a particularly effective way to disrupt your enemy's chariot charge was to release a mare in heat to run among the stallions pulling the chariots. This would throw the horses into pandemonium. The verse thus says simply that his beloved is profoundly exciting to him. Such an explanation may not carry a lot of spiritual weight, but people do like to learn such tidbits.

Another example: Yohanan Muffs of the Jewish Theological Seminary points out that according to ancient Middle Eastern literature, if an Egyptian father was childless and wanted to adopt a son, he would go into the slave market, select an heir, and say to him, "I shall be to you as a father and you shall be to me as a son." He would then free the slave and give him a patrimony. It is within this context that we should understand the phrase in Exodus 6:7: "And I will take you to me for a people, and I will be to you as God... and you shall know that I am the Lord your God who brings you out from under burdens of Egypt. And I will bring you into the land which I swore to give to Abraham, Isaac and Jacob and I will give it to you for a heritage."

God goes into the Egyptian slave market, adopts the people of Israel and gives them a patrimony. That is to say, the Torah spoke in the metaphors of its time in such a way that the relationship between God and the people of Israel made sense to the people.

The story David and Goliath can be viewed not only as triumph of good over evil, or of the brave over the strong, but also as a description of the power of technology. Bows were not characteristically used by Philistine warriors. For medium ranges they used something like a hurling javelin. When David used his sling, he was therefore out-ranging the weapons of Goliath. (*The Art of Warfare in Biblical Lands,* Yigal Yadin, McGraw-Hill).

With that thought as background, you could talk about the importance of using modern technology to bring our Jewish institutions up to date. Sincerity by itself won't carry us. Though our values may be ancient, the instruments we use to convey them need not be. Reading in the secondary biblical, archaeological and historical literature like Nahum Sarna's *Understanding Genesis* and *Exploring Exodus* (Schocken), in addition to the *Biblical Archeology Reader* (Anchor Books/Doubleday), can provide you with such insights.

The *Anchor Bible* (Doubleday) is another possible source for this kind of material, but there are dozens of books and articles that could be suggested. Wander through your local synagogue or even public library and you will probably find quite a few.

A word of caution; Don't get too carried away with the idea that the Bible is a history book. It is also a history book, but it is not only or even primarily that. Instead, it is a religious book that wants to tell us about the relationship of God to the people of Israel. You should never let that fact out of your head as you prepare your d'var Torah.

The Creative Process

Some people can read everything, search their souls, and still end up without a d'var Torah. Furthermore, even those who are used to preparing such things get stuck from time to time. I sometimes find that I can sit with a Torah text in from of me, look at the pages until all of the lines begin to squiggle, and not a single hint of an idea worth communicating emerges.

It doesn't take too long to end up in complete paralysis and panic. When that happens, consider the following plan of attack: It is very hard to force certain kinds of literary productivity. In these cases, an indirect assault often works much better that a frontal one. This is why you should read the text well in advance of when you're going to have to speak, weeks in advance, if possible. Try to look at it immediately after you have accepted your assignment.

Something may strike your fancy. One or two issues may jump out of the *parashah* and demand "Interpret me!" On the spot, write out any of the ideas that occur to you at that first reading. This is important because your first reaction may in the end provide you with your best ideas. Having looked at the text, even if only quickly, put it down but not away. Worry about it, but not too much.

For the next several weeks keep the *parashah* in your consciousness at a low level of energy. Look at the text a few more times if it is a tough one, or perhaps look at it with some of the commentaries. But avoid sitting down and slaving over it. Instead, go about your usual business. During this time, ideas will whir around in the back of you head. Then somehow, something happens. A friend says the magic words, a magazine article evokes the right association, or some phrase jumps off the page of the Bible and suddenly you know just what you want to say.

A slightly souped-up variant of this method is to read the text carefully just before bed. Then go to sleep without trying to work out the problem. Keep paper and pencil by your bed. You will be surprised how often you will get the answer you are looking for either in the middle of the night or early the next morning just before you get up. The insight comes neither from the text nor your head and feelings, but in the interplay between them.

This percolation time is an essential part of the process. Your d'var Torah may come together in the shower or while you're waiting for the bus. Keep your eyes and ears open and as if out of nowhere, things will fall into place. It won't happen without preparation, but once you have prepared, just relax and trust the process. The Force, whatever it is, will be with you. Don't ask me why it works. I don't know. I can't promise that it will work for you; maybe it won't. But I have read enough on the subject to be sure that the technique is not unique to me. Give it a chance. Allow yourself to fall free and let something deep inside you take over. If it happens, you may find, as I have, that the same method can be used to work on all sorts of complex intellectual and personal problems.

Once you get into the writing, don't hesitate to put on paper every thought you have ever had that relates to the subject in question. Don't censor yourself or hold back a thing. But once you know what it is that you are going to do, be altogether merciless. Cut out everything you don't absolutely need to make your point. If in doubt, throw it out.

It was a good idea but doesn't quite fit? Save it. You may be able to use it some other time. But don't put it in a talk where it doesn't belong and where it distracts people from your real point. Ferocious editing generally contributes far more to a good talk than great learning or creativity.

General Issues

The Torah text is the common ground between you and your listeners. They assume that you will find something in that text that will be worth their while to hear. They are not expecting to learn about the political situation in Israel or what was in the *New York Review of Books* last week. Neither are they expecting you to explicate the Torah in a way which is not at all congruent with their sense of the tradition. They anticipate hearing some old ideas or familiar verses in a new way that will invigorate their Jewish lives.

This means that you may not turn a text on its head by teaching for example, that Esau or Amalek, for some interesting reason that you have just discovered, are splendid fellows. You may conclude that Joseph is selfish and that David has serious personal flaws; the Torah knows that and agrees with you.

But you may not announce that Goliath is a misunderstood hero or that it is unreasonable to pick on poor Pharaoh who was really a kind and gentle man—at least not unless you want to alienate your listeners. You must work, even if loosely, within the traditional understanding of the character and events of the Bible. A d'var Torah, though it involves learning and challenge for the listener, also has a ritualistic quality. At some level it must provide comfort.

Not everyone accepts that proposition. There is a kind of person, often inexperienced, for whom making other Jews angry is a source of joy. They usually declare how pleased they are to be making others think. Instead of calling attention to Torah, which is the appropriate task, what they really do is call attention to themselves. Those who must listen to such speakers will always feel shortchanged.

Try not to get carried away by your conclusions, clever though they may be. You will generally be better served if you are modest about your claims. Ours is a very long and complex tradition, and there are very few propositions which can be stated flat-out without lots of qualifications. Any sentence which starts by saying "Judaism teaches that..." probably ought to make your listeners a little nervous. It is less pretentious and more honest to note that "Rabbi X teaches that... " or that "It is possible to interpret the text in the following manner."

If you can speak from notes, rather that a text, your d'var Torah will have freshness about it that cannot come from a read text. One option is an index card with no more than five separate entries of one line each.

But far better a read text than sloppiness or talking too long. Verbosity and bluffing are usually part of the same package. Inadequate preparation is one of the most frequent reasons people talk too long. It is usually more work to be brief. But even if your brevity is not the product of thoroughness or wisdom, a brief bad talk is always appreciated more than a long one. Also, the more dubious the methodology, the briefer your comments should be. That you are bluffing with a Snuff Box may be perfectly apparent to everyone, but people will be more forgiving if your talk is short.

There is almost no such thing as too short a d'var Torah. Don't even be afraid of one liners or quick insights into two or three verses of the *parashah*. If you can hang them all together, so much the better, but if you can't it is not serious. For some reason, groups of three often work well and provide a certain reassuring symmetry. If you can make three points or give three examples, your d'var Torah will feel complete regardless of how brief it is.

If the material you have been presenting is sufficiently suggestive, there is nothing wrong with letting people finish what you are saying inside their heads. More plants have died of overwatering than from thirst and more Jews have been turned off by talks that are too long than by those that have been too short or too evocative.

In my view, it is not necessary for a d'var Torah to be excessively earnest. You should not be a stand-up comedian, but a jigger of wry is rarely out of place. Gentle humor, if it is not overdone, helps put your listeners on your side. It makes them more ready to listen to the other things you have to say.

If you are really new at this sort of thing, giving your d'var Torah may be a terrifying experience. Your listeners do not want to know that. Cover your fears as best you can and help people sitting in front of you to relax. Knowing that they are in safe hands, they will listen better.

Some Resources That Are Available To You

Where should you look for your ideas? It should come as no shock that at the first stage in your preparation you should read the Torah portion for the week. If nothing happens after a first reading, head for the commentaries. But know in advance that many of the classics will be of no help to you.

If you find boring some kinds of Jewish literature that are to reputed to be great, it may be that you have not stretched your mind or spirit sufficiently. It is also possible that your response is right on target. Even though a book may have been written by a very great thinker or may once have been a great book, if the author is answering questions that we or our communities are not asking, those answers won't do much good in a d'var Torah.

The Hertz *Pentateuch and Haftorahs* (Soncino, London) is of course quite useful, although it will not provide you with clever things to quote. Since everyone who is sitting in front of you probably has the same witty insights immediately available on his or her lap, that tends to cheapen the coin a little. On the other hand, one of Hertz's insights may well send you off in an interesting direction.

His remarks may seem excessively apologetic in tone, but if you keep in mind that the was writing at the time of the rise of Nazi anti-Semitism, it is easy to forgive him and appreciate what he was trying to do. If Hertz doesn't work, try Rashi. Rashi is mainly interested in answers to questions he finds in the text, questions that you probably didn't even notice.

His answers are almost never useful for a contemporary d'var Torah, but his questions are. Trying to figure out what problem Rashi is trying to solve can yield some very interesting issues. The important thing he and the other commentators can do for you is force you to slow down and look at the text more carefully than you are likely to be able to do by yourself.

To assume that the Torah is written as casually as the *New York Times* is a great mistake. Rashi will keep you from trying to speed-read Torah.

For example, in Genesis. 1:1, Rashi tells us that the Torah begins with the creation of the world, rather than, as we might expect, with the history of the Jewish people. Why? Rashi's answer: So that when the nations will say that the Land of Israel belongs to them, we will have a record which says that determination was made by the Sovereign of all Creation, who gave the Land of Israel to the Jewish people.

Now it seems perfectly reasonable to most of us that the Torah should begin with the creation story. But Rashi makes us realize that this is not at all self-evident. If he has gotten us to see that, he may have also caused us to notice how very appropriate his response is to his times, the period of the first Crusades, when both Moslems and Christians were making claims on a land that we thought belonged to us.

The argument has rather modern ring to it. We may start to think about who really does own land, whether in Israel or anywhere else; and if we are that far along, Rashi has been a smashing success.

If you are just starting out, don't try to study the Rashi for the entire *parashah*. You may get bogged down in the details. Like a miner, choose a section that looks promising, then dig in and see if you can find treasure.

Besides Hertz and Rashi, there are other popular commentaries. In addition to the Hertz, the Soncino Press publishes what it calls *The Soncino Chumash*, which is an anthology of classic rabbinic commentaries to the Torah. I personally find them to be more technical than evocative and do not use the book very often.

M. Kasher's *Biblical Encyclopedia* (in Hebrew it is called *Torah Shelemah*, Jerusalem and N.Y.) includes just about everything. It is extraordinarily comprehensive and may even overwhelm you. Even though it is not complete, it includes too many volumes for the average private library. Check to see if some Jewish institution in your town has a copy.

The new *Jewish Publication Society Torah Commentary*, edited by Nahum Sarna, is particularly accessible, both intellectually and as an item that can easily be purchased in Jewish book stores. It is a useful balance of the scholarly and the sermonic.

I think the Artscroll Bible publications currently on the market are hopelessly pious and of no interest at all. In these books it is impossible to distinguish between the Midrashic meaning of the text and its straightforward meaning, impossible because the editors seem to be committed to a position which denies the existence of any such distinction. I have yet to find anything they want to teach me that I want to know. Because the series is such a good idea and in such a splendid format, it is a double shame that the product is so bad.

Thought it has some similarities that put me off, a far more promising collection is *The Torah Anthology* (Maznaim, N.Y.), Aryeh Kaplan's translation of an 18th Century Sephardi collection called *Me'am Lo'ez*.

Ramban (Nachmanides) Commentary on the Torah has been translated into English by Charles Chavel (Shilo, N.Y.). Ramban's ideas are often wonderful, but he is very verbose and sometimes you can die waiting to get to them. A taste for Ramban has to be cultivated.

The standard Hasidic commentaries usually leave me cold as well, particularly if they explain the human and devine psyche in terms of the *Sephirot*, the Kabbalistic system which tries to show how an infinite God is able to relate to a world of finite matter. I never like the way they dissolve the text and de-historicize it to make it mean something altogether different from what it says. Friends whose judgment I otherwise trust tell me that I am way off-base in this matter and there is very rich material to be found in these sources. I am not so sure, but perhaps you shouldn't take my word on this one.

I react differently to Hasidic stories, which often do speak to me. They are much more suggestive than the regular Hasidic commentaries and leave me more room to play and develop ideas. Some of the story collections are arranged according to the portions of the week. In this category I recommend a nice little book called *Al Hatorah* by Rabbi Mordecai Hacohen (Orot, Jerusalem). There are probably some English equivalents, but I am not familiar with any.

There are two collections with modern sensibilities that I recommend very highly, one in English, the other in Hebrew; *Wellsprings of Torah* by Alexander Zusia Friedman (Judaica Press, N.Y.) and *Meotzrayneu Hayashan* by B. Yeushson [Moshe Justman] (Maariv, Jerusalem).

These anthologies, which contain both Hasidic and non-Hasidic material, were popular in prewar Europe—and deservedly so. Another set of volumes that is similar in tone to these two is *Ituray Torah* by A .Y. Greenberg (Yavneh, Jerusalem). It works over much of the same material as the other two and is a fine substitute for either of them.

The Torah; A Modern Commentary (UAHC, N.Y.) prepared by Gunther Plaut for Reform congregations is definitely worth trying. The notes are good, and every time I have used the very engaging section called Gleanings, I have been well rewarded. I don't like the way the *parashot* are broken up, but I have learned how to find my way.

One of the early places to look is either the *Encyclopedia Judaica*, the new one, or the *Jewish Encyclopedia*, the old one printed in 1901. While there have been many significant innovations in biblical criticism, philology and archeology since that time, most of the events recorded in the Bible took place before 1901. So if you ever come across a *Jewish Encyclopedia* in used book store, snap it up at once. (There is a reprint edition that is floating around which costs more and does not have the wonderful old color prints that are to be found in the front of each volume.) The new encyclopedia is also rather inexpensive these days.

You will almost never get a d'var Torah from these encyclopedias. What they will do for you is keep you from saying dumb things. They will prevent you from placing events in the wrong country or the wrong millennium. They will provide you with the consensus of scholarly opinion about the subject that interest you.

They will tell you about the biblical and rabbinic views of particular biblical figures. If the biblical subjects you are working on seems really mixed up, the encyclopedia will either agree that it is mixed up or will clear things up for you.

The books I have listed should by no means be considered definitive. They reflect my prejudices which you may not share. Besides, new books appear all the time. Keep a lookout for any that might engage you.

Whatever source you consult, don't worry about stealing an idea. If you state it in the name of its originator, you cease to be a thief; you merely become erudite. You do not need to invent an idea all by yourself. As a matter of fact, unless you are very special, if you have invented it yourself there is a good chance that it is misguided or wrong. What is mostly likely to happen when you find that someone else's idea is appealing that you will work it into your own thoughts in such a way that, by the time you are finished, the original author wouldn't even want to claim credit for it.

Among the most overlooked sources for idea are your own life experiences. There are themes that are so much a part of you that barely know they are there. How can you find them? In your stories.

There are stories that most of us tell and tell rather often. Our friends and spouses can see them coming from a mile away: "Oh, not that one again!" There is a very good chance that your stories illustrate issues that strike you as particularly interesting or important, and that are very likely dealt with in the Torah.

As you look over a text, keep those stories reasonably close to the front of the file cabinet in your head.

Example: Back in the mid-fifties, I was serving as rabbi in Bombay. From time to time it amused me to think of myself as the Chief Rabbi of India, Ceylon and Tibet. (That is to say, there weren't any other rabbis around.)

The Jews outside of Bombay lived in isolated villages. Since these people were rarely visited by outsiders, I took a trip by oxcart to see them. What I had not counted on was that word had gone before our little party that a "famous" American rabbi was coming to address them. The entire community came in from the nearby villages, assembled in the synagogue and waited to be charmed by my golden tongue.

I have always extemporized badly. If I have time to prepare, I can do well enough, but I have always been jealous of those folks who can give a brilliant speech at the drop of a biblical verse. When asked to speak without preparation, I will generally decline.

But it was clear on this occasion that declining was simply not an option. I opened the Bible in the front of the synagogue to the week's *parashah* and on the spot I put together a d'var Torah. I was in luck. The Spirit moved me. I warmed to the task and instead of giving my usual dry, restrained little talk, I positively orated. When it was all over, it was clear that people loved it. They stamped and whistled and made wonderful whooping noises. I was delighted. In one day, I had learned how to do something I had not been able to accomplish after years of trying.

Feeling good about a job well done, I got up to leave. As my companions and I neared the door, our host stopped me apologetically and asked if we would please wait and not leave just yet. "You only need to stay until I translate the speech," he said. "No one here understands any English."

This is a story I love to tell on myself. Once when I was called upon to speak on the *parashah* that included the verse "Do not curse the deaf"

(Lev. 19:14), it finally occurred to me what had happened in that little synagogue. I addressed my own needs rather that those of the people I was supposed to be addressing. In the light of the anecdote, I suggested that this verse could be understood to mean that it is inappropriate to tell people what they are unable to hear.

A Concluding Caution

You should know about an important aspect of giving a d'var Torah that is quite unsettling. You can work very hard on a talk only to find that it falls on deaf ears. On the other hand, you can whip up a little something that morning and discover that it saves someone's soul.

It is more than slightly bewildering to have a couple tell you ten years later how this or that d'var Torah that you gave changed the direction of their lives, saved their marriage, or convinced their son to return to Jewish life.

You may not remember who they are or what it was you said, even though you feel sure it couldn't have been what they heard. I mention this because teaching Torah is real responsibility. People are often quite open and vulnerable on a Shabbat morning. Once you send out your words, you never know just what use people will make of them. So be sure they are the words you want to say.

Giving a d'var Torah should not primarily serve to feed your own ego, although it may do that too. It should be an attempt to perform a holy act, and it is within that context that you should make your preparations. If you keep that in mind you may find personal pleasure and growth among the by-products of your efforts. You may even become a great Torah teacher.

Hospitality Should be Practiced Religiously

W hen I was a kid, it was characteristic that our family never had a lot of guests. We didn't have much space at home and, but more to the point, a home was thought to be a rather closed corporation. Forty years ago in Safed, a friend and I were desperately looking for a hotel room late one Friday afternoon. There were none to be found. A young schoolteacher, whom I remember today only as Judah, witnessed our consternation as we vainly sought accommodations. He approached us and said, "It is unthinkable that Jews should be without a place to stay on Shabbat. You will come home with me." That was when I began to learn about *hakhnasat or̲h̲im*— the traditional mitzvah of bringing guests into the house.

Since that time, my life was saved by a Jewish doctor who took me into his home in southern India when I was very ill with boils; I was invited home for lunch by a lady in Rome because she heard me speaking Hebrew; as a student, I schnorred my way across the country never paying for lodging because there was always the home of a friend of a friend of a friend with whom I could stay.

I could multiply the stories endlessly. I will never be able to reciprocate these people's hospitality. All that I can do is give to guests what some other hosts have given to me and hope that they will do the same for others.

We seem to get two kinds of guests. The less gratifying are usually the people who just got stuck and need a place to stay overnight or for a few days. They never come from the same place twice and each guest's story is unlike the preceding one. If you want to continue to enjoy such people over a period of time, don't flutter over them too much. Chat as long as you find that good things are happening between you, and then only if you are not pressed with other urgent responsibilities.

Beyond that, show them where the linens are, let them stow their belongings, and point out what's around for breakfast. When the time comes, they'll be on their way. We try to apply these rules uniformly to friends of our kids, visiting dignitaries and miscellaneous wayfarers.

Perhaps we have been fortunate, but we have almost never been seriously imposed on by our guests. In general, our guests have given us far more than we have given them.

We find that we generally "specialize" in a second variety of guests—guests for Shabbat and holidays. At these times we are not pressed by outside concerns and can really be present to enjoy and learn from those who come into our home.

Somewhere I read that children who live in homes that house boarders are more adaptable and better adjusted that those that live only within their nuclear families. I realize that the causal factors producing such data may not have a simple explanation, but I have enough data from the life of our own family to know how much my wife, our children, and I have gained from those who have come into our home.

Over the years they have included hundreds of students and faculty, mostly from the days when I was Hillel Foundation director at Yale. Now it is primarily friends we have a chance to meet in any number of casual ways. We invite people we would like to know better, people we suspect might be feeling lonely, people who will bring us special joy, people who would like to learn something about Shabbat or Yom Tov (the holidays), people who know really good Shabbat songs, neighbors, people who just drop in and people for whom we can find no particular rationale at all.

Every now and then we get a few duds—guests who pretend that they are visiting anthropologists come to watch our quaint oriental rites. We are also burdened with a problem that many readers of this book happily will not face: those people who are terrified by being in the house of a rabbi for the first time in their lives. They don't know how they are "supposed" to act and are sure that they will inadvertently do something dreadfully gauche.

If they are sufficiently on edge, there is really very little we can do except heave the same sigh of relief that they do once they are out the door. Far more often, however, we have fun. We have learned about different kinds of people, different parts of the country or the world; we have learned of the activities of long-lost friends through the "Do you know...?" game. Our children have met new styles of Jewishness. (It is our children, in fact, who have usually been most disappointed when we do not have guests).

Guests have picked us up when we were in the doldrums. If there were squabbles afoot anywhere in the family, the presence of outsiders often forced us to behave for a while and frequently took enough edge off the incident that started the trouble that we could reestablish contact with much greater ease than would otherwise have been possible. Even the "company behavior" of children was a nice thing (although we couldn't count on it consistently—alas).

Hakhnasat Orḥim

We have developed some guidelines for ourselves over the years:

Offers of hospitality should always be given wholeheartedly and with sincerity. That is—if you don't mean it, don't say it. If you don't want them, don't invite them.

Sometimes, for very good reasons, people to whom you would like to open up your home simply cannot accept your offer. For their comfort and your own, drop the subject.

No one family member should be stuck with the whole project. When you have guests, the whole family should try to prepare for them. Otherwise, the burden will fall on too few members of the family, who may not only be too busy to enjoy guests but may even come to resent them.

There is no reason for not enlisting the help of guests in clearing away food, cleaning up the dishes and the like. It usually makes them feel more relaxed about being with you and makes your life a little easier too. You don't need to dread what you will be stuck with when the company leaves. It also brings the evening to a definitive close. One of the things we like about Shabbat entertaining is that it has a beginning, a middle and an end. There is no dreadful uncertainty about whether the company will catch on about when it is appropriate to go home.

Try to avoid a trap I fall into too frequently. I come rushing home at the last minute and pull a Clark Kent, flinging off my workaday frenetics to zip into my fresh Super-Jew Shabbat clothes and mood. It never works.

One way to keep your hospitality from becoming burdensome is to keep the food simple. We find that we prefer to offer straightforward, uncomplicated cooking to many guests rather than Cordon Bleu goodies to only a select few.

Do not overdo! By the end of spring we sometimes feel ourselves "overguested." We want to have a bit more privacy for our family. Then it is time to stop for a few weeks or even for the season. Come fall, we will begin to feel the things have been too quiet and that we are once again ready to fulfill the mitzvah of *hakhnasat orḥim*.

On Baldness and The Jewish Problem

ny bald man who has ever tried to wear a yarmulke (skullcap) knows the problem. The yarmulke won't stay put. Bobby pins or the Israeli clips for people with hair don't help—there is nothing to attach

them to. You can't bow your head down for the *Aleinu* prayer or look up to see if there are stars at the end of Shabbat before *Havdalah* without losing your lid. Try to dance at a wedding and you find yourself dancing with one hand placed firmly on the top of your head. Some men quickly begin to consider desperate alternatives like staples or Crazy Glue—or secularism—or *streimels*, the big fur hats the Hasidim wear. Others, unable to keep them in place, whose yarmulkes are seldom on their heads but always on their minds, develop a yarmulke tic, forever reaching up to put the little rascal back in place.

But fear not. You no longer need to be concerned. Advanced technology can save the day! Forget about black taffeta, or Israeli crocheted yarmulkes. Buy a leather or suede one that has some nap on the inside, wet it briefly but thoroughly and pop it on your shiny head, nappy side down. It will attach itself with the tenacity of a barnacle. Now, you will be able to prostrate yourself on Yom Kippur, dance with abandon on Simhat Torah, do yoga exercises upside down, or even run a marathon, and your yarmulke will not fall off. In fact, the greater the expenditure of energy, the better it will stick, for your head sweat glues it down.

The only thing you cannot do in a wet leather yarmulke is swim (or go to the mikveh), for the additional water will break the seal and your yarmulke will float away. Also—don't use the ones that are deeply colored, unless you are partial to a maroon or blue-dyed skull. My own preference is not for the suede yarmulkes with cloth edging, which wears out, but rather for the all soft-leather versions in neutral colors, which are a little harder to find.

I am certain that they will wear for at least ten years, but for all I know, they could last a lifetime. By the way, be careful to wet your yarmulke only in the privacy of your own home. If your friends see you pouring drinking water into your yarmulke, as some (former) friends once did me, they may begin to raise serious questions about you.

One of my favorite Bible stories, one that is usually censored out of the Jewish school curriculum, is the tale in which Elisha the prophet is provoked by youngsters who taunt him for being bald.

Elisha proceeds to call some bears out of the forest who immediately eat up forty-two nasty children (II Kings 2:23-24). The rabbis of the Talmud say it never really happened like that. As for me? I would rather like to believe that it did. After all, even bald prophets are entitled to a little respect.

But if Elisha had known about leather yarmulkes, the whole story might never have been told, for no one would have realized just how bald he was if, instead of falling off or sliding around, his yarmulke had been stuck firmly in place.

One can only wonder about how many other significant events in our history took place at the drop of a hat.

Eating, Not Eating and Drinking

Jewish Haute Cuisine

Or

Kosher In The Clouds

Frankly, keeping kosher can be a pain in the neck. Every time I take a bite to eat, I have to worry about an incredible number of arbitrary rules.

Meat and milk products at the same meal are a no-no and there have to be separate dishes for each. The only four-legged animals I can eat have to have split hooves and chew their cud. Most conventional fowl are all right but they can't have been killed in the hunt. They, as well as the other animals, have to be slaughtered according to very precise regulations which minimize the animal's pain. After having been slaughtered, they must subsequently be inspected. Permissible fish must have fins and scales. Nothing like eels or crabs that creep or slither along the floor of the ocean will do. During the week of Passover there are additional prohibitions. In addition to those normally observed, no food made with leaven is allowed. And this is just the beginning.

Some of these regulations are edifying enough or at least have edifying implications, but a lot of them, on the face of it at least, seem rather silly. But it turns out that these apparently arbitrary laws make a very important contribution to my Jewish religious consciousness. Nowhere is this clearer than when trying to keep kosher on airplanes since regular airline food won't do.

When I started observing the kosher food rules, I viewed my decision to do so as a very private one, something between me and the Holy One. It did not occur to me that if you want to keep kosher at 30,000 feet, a lot of other people are involved as well. I ordered my first kosher airline meal through my travel agent when I purchased my ticket and then promptly forgot about it. It was a startling reminder of my obligations to several thousand years of Jewish tradition when a voice came over the airplane loud speaker. "Would passenger Israel with the kosher meal please identify himself?" After I timidly raised my hand, I waited for the stewardess to come over and pin on my big yellow star. What I discovered at that moment was that keeping kosher is a public Jewish declaration that carries with it a series of heavy responsibilities.

There are Jews who keep kosher at home, but not when eating out. They often explain themselves saying that though they are not really religious, they want to make at statement about Jewish community values with their kosher homes. They have it backwards. The place you make a community statement is when you keep kosher out. At the airport ticket counter I ask the clerk if my kosher meal has been put aboard. (It has been forgotten or sent to the wrong flight more than once.) The clerk consults the computer and assures me that everything is fine. I then remember that I need some money and ask if I can cash a check. "No, it is contrary to airline policy...but wait, you just ordered a kosher meal. I can certainly trust you. Don't make it too large a check though. I'll get into trouble."

I had labeled myself someone who was committed to religious ritual and whether I liked it or not, I now had to be committed to religious ethics as well. That airline clerk was betting her job on my religious rectitude. My tradition and I were both on the line. I guess that is exactly what is supposed to happen to me and is what it means that I am obligated to sanctify God's name with my life. Both my own and my God's reputation were at stake. I didn't realize I was getting into all that by ordering some overcooked chicken. I hoped the check wouldn't bounce.

The plane was late in taking off. As a consolation prize, the stewardess came by with free drinks. She noticed my kosher meal order. "I guess you won't be having an alcoholic beverage."

Wait a minute. That was good Scotch that was receding down the airplane aisle. As far as she was concerned, if you eat "religious food" you don't drink alcohol. But she's wrong. Scotch has nothing to do with keeping kosher. In my books Scotch is a lot less menacing than the pork or lobster on the menu, which are really dangerous. She wants to turn me into a kosher Southern Baptist. There is hardly time to discuss the theology of it all as she rolls by with her little cart. Do I stop her and tell her I want the drink, thereby forcing her reconsider her religious categories and think about mine? Do I pass it up so that I not appear in her eyes as a hypocrite? What I discover is that the act of keeping kosher demands far more religious engagement than I ever could have anticipated.

Few matters test my religious sensibilities and my patience more than the other passengers who steal my meals. If the stewardess doesn't know who ordered the kosher meals and asks over the intercom, almost invariably a passenger who wanted a kosher meal but forgot to order it, who used to eat kosher meals twenty years ago and has decided to try again...just this once, or who has heard that kosher meals are better than the regular ones...such a person raises his hand and I am left without breakfast. As he munches away happily, I wait for my food. I wait and wait and wait. After a while, the stewardess discovers that there aren't any more kosher meals since someone else has taken my meal "by mistake." The stewardess reassures me. If I would like the bacon and eggs instead, she would be happy to bring them. I am not reassured.

I glare at my seat-mate. He smiles back at me. "I grew up in an Orthodox home," he says. "Haven't had a kosher meal in a long time. Didn't know you could get them on airplanes. It sure is a new world. My mother would never have believed it. This is terrific. I should get one more often. Have you ever tried one? Oh, you keep kosher too? You really do it all the time? Tell me why. It is a shame they don't have a meal for you." I mumble to myself, "Just my luck. Today you have to decide to keep kosher, on my breakfast, when I am starved!"

We talk. He really wants to have a serious conversation. We discuss what it means to try to turn eating into a religious act. What is my responsibility to the calf that I eat or to the potato? Can I do what I will with the produce of the earth? Does God really care how many hours I wait between drinking milk and eating meat? I can't even figure out a decent way to make him feel guilty. Now I carry a little bag of granola with me whenever I take a meal flight, to be safe.

Kosher meals used to be a lot better than the regular airline meals. (On a few airlines, they still are.) The rumor among kosher eating passengers is that too many people began to eat them, including both Jewish and non-Jewish passengers who ate kosher meals only on airplanes. Since they cost more, the airlines wanted to discourage that practice so that only the passengers who had no alternative would order them. Now, you really have to have a religious mandate or a very specialized taste for bland brisket to enjoy kosher food on an airplane, because that is all you are likely to get. It is kosher, but it is also rather boring eating.

In hopes of having something a little more exciting, from time to time, I have ordered a vegetarian meal instead of a kosher one. Since the kosher food rules mostly have to do with meat, there isn't much in a vegetable that isn't kosher. For a while that went well, but then airplane veggie dinners began turning out to be two apples and a carrot or a dish of celery sticks and a tomato. They drew no distinction between vegetarians and rabbits. The European and Asian airlines know what to do with a vegetable, but not the Americans. I went back to kosher.

A few years ago, I had occasion to be flying during the week of Passover. When my kosher meal arrived, I noticed that it contained food products like bread and noodles which are permitted throughout the rest of the year but are prohibited during the Passover holiday. Closer inspection revealed that though it was indeed a kosher meal, it was not kosher for Passover.

"Stewardess", I announced. "I can't eat this meal. I ordered a kosher meal. This one isn't kosher."

"But sir," she said, "it says on the wrapper that it is kosher." Then I had my moment of secret revenge on that hapless stewardess for all those raw carrots, for those meals stolen by other passengers, for the Scotch that whizzed by me too quickly for debate.

"Last week this meal was kosher," I declared. "Next week it will be kosher. But this week, it isn't kosher."

Then I went back to my newspaper. This time, let the stewardess do the theology.

Fast Food

Fasting is no fun. It isn't supposed to be. Nevertheless, fasting is said to have salutary effects and is therefore held in high esteem by many religious traditions and health regimens. In the Jewish tradition fasting is taken quite seriously and so we find that on a major holy day like Yom Kippur, even Jews who wouldn't think of entering a synagogue will nevertheless fast because they believe fasting to be good for either the body or the spirit or both.

In the Jewish religious tradition, the discomfort that is produced by fasting is thought to have instructional value and is intended to help us reflect on our human frailty. This does not mean that Jews are intended to make themselves as miserable as possible on Yom Kippur, only that they not eat or drink. The discomfort some people experience during a fast is so extreme that they forget the appropriate agendas for the day. It is possible to diminish that discomfort without losing awareness of the fast.

Not only is eating wisely tricky, so is fasting wisely. Here are some strategies that may make the fast a little easier.

This may be hard to believe after one is twenty or so hours into a fast, but most healthy adults can survive well over a month without eating. Most of the unpleasantness associated with a fast does not come from lack of food, but rather, from lack of fluid. The solution therefore is to super-hydrate beforehand. "Camel up" before a fast, drinking a great deal the prior afternoon, perhaps two quarts well in advance of your final pre-fast meal. At the time you may feel you are going to float away. Before the fast is over, you will be glad you did it. Diluted orange juice is a good drink, so is water. Beer or other alcoholic beverages will dehydrate you.

Though you should drink a lot before a fast, you do not need to stuff yourself with food. Eat a normal meal but emphasize carbohydrates like potato or noodle dishes, not proteins or fats. Carbohydrates bond with water which your body can "drink" when it needs to during your fast. Proteins do not. Most of the dramatic but limited weight loss that people on high protein diets experience is lost water that protein molecules cannot hold onto or bring into your system, water that you want around during a fast.

I have heard of grandmothers in Europe who fed their families immense starch meals for the better part of the week before a fast and then, at the final meal encouraged everyone to eat heavy meat dishes. The carbohydrates taken early would provide the necessary water reservoir. The last-minute meat meal would give the comfort of a full stomach for a number of hours. What people who still eat this way before a fast have to consider is whether they really want to take on all those calories. This kind of pre-fast diet might have been suitable for a culture in which meat was a rarity and people were close to involuntary fasting through much of the year. It is not clear that it makes sense in ours.

Fast food does not need to be hopelessly bland, but go easy on the salt, which may make you thirsty. Season with non-irritating spices and herbs.

The nausea and headaches that many people fasting report have nothing to do either with food or fluid. They are usually the result of caffeine withdrawal. If you are a heavy coffee or cola drinker, start tapering off a week or so before the fast. Unless you drink a great deal of caffeine, one cup less a day, with the day before the fast being caffeine free, will usually do it. Using decaffeinated coffee during this period may help you fool your system. Caffeine withdrawal symptoms are less of a problem when you are eating and drinking than when fasting.

A brief fast is not a quick weight-loss scheme. An average adult will burn 2,000 to 2,500 calories, about two-thirds of a pound, during a twenty-four hour fast. It doesn't take long at all to put that back on again. A couple of pieces of cheesecake and you will be just about even. Most of the weight loss that you see on the scale for the day or two after a fast is fluid that you will quickly replace.

After the fast, be careful not to gorge yourself. Since the body protects itself from starvation when you are not eating by slowing down the rate at which it burns food, the calories you take on right after a fast will stay with you a lot longer than those acquired when your metabolism is once again functioning at full speed.

These suggestions will not prevent you from experiencing the fast. If you are not eating or drinking for twenty-four to twenty-six hours, there is no chance you will forget that you are fasting. But it is important for you to be able to focus on some soul-searching and prayer, rather than on your complaining stomach.

So prepare yourself for fasting, both physically and spiritually, and in the words of one of the traditional pre-fast greetings, have an easy fast!

Why Jewish Wine Tastes Terrible

ews have no reason to be ashamed of Jewish cooking. It isn't designed to appeal to the eye as French cooking is, and it may not be as subtle as Northern Italian cooking, but to a serious eater, Jewish food competes well with the best.

So why is it that Jewish wine is almost always dreadful? Is it etched on a tablet somewhere that is has to taste either like grape syrup or wine vinegar? How is it that Jews are grateful when a wine critic writes "pleasant for a kosher wine"? Perhaps one of the reasons there have been so few Jewish alcoholics until recent years is that for generations, the only wine Jews had to drink tasted awful. It is hard to develop a taste for wine if one is limited to Jewish wine.

I am always amazed to see an Italian or a Frenchman sit down to dinner and finish off a bottle of wine that would put me under the table. Two glasses, and I am out of business. That is often rather characteristic of Jewish drinking. Certainly in generations past, the average "wine drinking" Jew would have had one drink of wine to formally welcome and sanctify the Shabbat on Friday night and another to bid it farewell with the Havdalah ceremony on Saturday night and would then put the wine away for a week. But if after two glassfuls, you put the cork back in and return the bottle to the shelf for another week, by the time you reopen the bottle, you are likely to find not the fine wine with which you started but vinegar.

A good way to prevent spoilage, particularly if you don't have refrigeration, is to add a lot of sugar to the wine. Yeast cannot survive in a very sweet medium and the wine retains its sugary drinkability for a long time. It may not be wine according to the standards of most wine drinkers, but it isn't vinegar either, thus the grape-syrup-called-wine product.

A second consideration is that the two major Jewish communities of the world today trace their origins to either eastern Europe or the Middle East. In neither location was there a wine-drinking culture. If Jews have been willing to settle for mediocre wine, it may well be because until recently our collective historic palate never knew any better. If Jews today are no longer satisfied with sweet syrup and are now drinking dry wine, it is a sure sign that we are finishing off the bottles and no longer drinking in the same modest quantities we used to. A Manischewitz Bordeaux or a Kedem Rhine Wine is as certain a measure of Jewish assimilation into the surrounding culture as we are likely to see.

Some theology and history are also necessary if we are to understand why Jewish wine generally tastes the way it does. To begin with: What, according to Jewish law, is Jewish wine, and what makes it kosher?

The term kosher means religiously fit or proper. It doesn't only refer to food. One does of course talk about kosher meat. That would be meat from a permissible animal that had been slaughtered properly, inspected for blemishes and disease and had the blood drawn out of it. But one could also speak of a kosher *sukkah,* that little shelter or booth that is built on the occasion of the fall harvest festival of Sukkot. A kosher sukkah would be one that is the right size, that has at least three walls and the proper leafy covering. You could even describe a person as kosher. When the texts speak of a kosher young woman, for example, they are referring to one characterized by piety, modesty and attentiveness to Jewish law.

Jewish law would require wine to have a particular set of characteristics in order to be considered kosher. First of all, it has to be kosher as a food. There are some European red wines to which animal blood is added for color. Any blood and certainly the blood of non-kosher animals would make wine non-kosher. To be kosher for Passover, wine must be made in leaven-free utensils and have no yeasts added, beyond those that enter from the air. But non-kosher additives are rare. They are not the usual problem that raises questions about whether wine is kosher.

The major concerns stem from an entirely different set of issues. They are the ancient and medieval rabbis' perceptions of the religions of the majority cultures in which they lived. The rabbis of the Talmud described three foods as potentially involved in idolatry: wine, bread and oil. These three were said to be used routinely as libations and offerings in the ritual practices of classical Roman religion. Were a Jew to purchase them from a Roman, there seemed to be a very real possibility that the Jew might unknowingly end up consuming food that had been used previously in idolatrous worship. Given the Jewish horror of idolatry, they were, therefore, put off limits.

With the passing of time, concern about using non-Jewish oil vanished and concerns about using non-Jewish bread diminished. But non-Jewish wine, probably because it was part of the public worship of a majority religion, Christianity, remained a drink prohibited to Jews. Jews only drank wine they had made themselves. The use of graven images in the church was very problematic for the rabbinic tradition. Sophisticated rabbis realized that sophisticated Christians were not offering wine to idols; nevertheless, the use of that wine in the presence of statues of one who was described as the Son of God never sat easily with Jews. Perhaps church intellectuals knew the statues weren't idols, but it was never clear to the Jews that all the peasants who prayed in front of those statues knew that.

The Moslems were easily as horrified by Christian images as were the Jews. It is not surprising that Maimonides, one of the major codifiers of Jewish law, who lived in a Moslem culture, declared Christians idolaters. Other rabbis who actually lived among Christians had a better idea of what they were about. Menahem Ha-Me'iri, a fourteenth century rabbi of Provence, and Moses Rivkes, a seventeenth century Lithuanian legal authority, felt that there was much that was positive in Christianity. But even rabbis who had more reservations about the

Christian tradition did not view Christians as the kind of idolaters the Talmud described and that is the view of most traditional Jewish legal authorities today.

Nevertheless, throughout the years there remained a deep-seated suspicion, particularly among observant eastern European Jews, about the nature of Christianity. Not only the hard-liners, but even the "liberals" did not think much of Christian forms of worship and had no desire to break down the social barriers between Jews and Christians. While non-Jewish wine (actually wine made by Christians, since wine was prohibited to Moslems) could not be suspected of being used in libations to idols, it still didn't seem right to drink it. Another principle, one that reaches back to the Talmud, is brought into play. Jews are told you may not drink non-Jewish wine, "so that you will not marry their daughters."

Shakespeare understood this impulse when he has Shylock say to the non-Jewish Bassanio, "I will buy with you, sell with you, talk with you, walk with you...but I will not eat with you, drink with you, nor pray with you." If Jews and non-Jews become comfortable enough with one another to be drinking partners, intermarriage is just around the corner. It is hard to say that such a view is mistaken.

Though such a law served the interests of Jewish continuity, it was probably hard to sustain. True, one could drink whiskey and beer with non-Jews without disobeying the law, but if you were doing business in a serious wine culture, as some Jews did, it must have been difficult to relate to non-Jews and never drink wine with them.

One way to get around the problem was to boil or spice the wine so that it wouldn't be wine any more. It might look like wine, and contain the amount of alcohol that is characteristic of wine and would more or less taste like wine, but in fact, it would really be something else. So if you think Jewish wine doesn't taste like wine, you are probably right. Most Jewish wine these days has been boiled to avoid that possibility. If you look carefully at the plastic sleeve around the stopper, the one that is removed before you open the bottle, you are likely to find the seldom translated Hebrew which tells you just that, *yayin m'vushal,* cooked wine.

Currently, there seem to be attempts to produce quality Jewish wine (the most successful of them by people who knew what good non-Jewish wine tasted like before they became observant Jews). I am also told that whole fleets of Hasidim now rent sections of European vineyards and take over the wine-making process using local grapes and production methods. I have not been fortunate enough to come upon a successful product of these new endeavors. Perhaps the really good vineyards aren't rented out or maybe the cooking does in the wine. It is my fear that when someone finally does make a first-rate kosher wine, it will probably turn out to be so expensive I won't be able to buy it anyway.

Thus, Jewish wine becomes kosher by not having non-kosher additives, and by being made by Jews, who are not generally thought to be idolaters. Then just to be safe, it is usually cooked so that it can't really be considered wine which could be spoiled if it somehow came into the hands of suspect non-Jews.

It is only quite recently that concerns about using non-Jewish wine have extended to other grape-related products like grape jelly and carbonated drinks with natural grape flavor. The assumption is that maybe they could have been made from something that could have been used for libations. No matter that the Jews of Italy, who were certainly as well located as anyone to know about Christianity and wine, never made their own wine or hesitated to drink non-Jewish wine. Never mind that Moses Isserles, the great Polish commentator on the *Shulḥan Arukh,* had no strong opposition to Jews drinking non-Jewish wine. But his comment to that effect only appeared in the first edition of his commentary.

When Jews start to worry about a subject, they worry a lot. The fact that a major authority said it was not prohibited carries very little weight among many observant Jews these days. After all, if we listened to everyone's leniencies, we could get ourselves into all sorts of trouble.

We are now in a situation in which the Jewish law regarding wine doesn't appear to work. In the Talmud, the rabbis tried to deal with the substantive issues. There were Talmudic authorities who believed that Jews not only shouldn't drink wine with non-Jews, neither should they drink beer nor hard liquor with them. Today, we have only preserved the wine prohibition, which prevents very few of the things it seems it was intended to prevent. The wine we aren't supposed to drink is clearly not being made by idolaters and whether or not we drink it will have little effect on whether or not we marry their daughters.

It is probably true that people who drink only kosher wine are less likely to intermarry than those who drink non-kosher wine, but that is more likely to flow from their general life style than this specific prohibition. That we may drink cooked wine with non-Jews, but not uncooked wine, drink soda pop made with artificial grape flavor, but not natural flavor, do not seem especially effective ways to place distance between non-Jews and ourselves, if that is our intention. What we have kept are the formal strictures of the law, unrelated to intent. They have taken on a life of their own. Given the way in which alcoholic beverages are used in this culture, perhaps Jewish law should become more stringent and prohibit us from drinking any alcoholic beverages with non-Jews. Alternatively, since it doesn't seem to accomplish anything in its present form and is ignored by many otherwise observant Jews, it might be argued that the prohibition should be ignored like the original prohibition against non-Jewish bread and oil.

The solution to the problem ought to be simple, but it isn't. It is all part of an issue that has been of concern to observant Jews for a long time. Is Jewish law supposed to make sense? Does it intend to achieve a particular purpose, or is it an inherited tradition to which we are obligated whether it seems sensible or not? If a law has an intention, in this case to keep us from intermarrying, then, if it no longer prevents intermarriage we will want to change or ignore it. If the law has no understandable intention, then if we accept it we do so because we are fulfilling our overall obligations to the covenant and for no other reason.

The discussion goes all the way back to King Solomon who is taught that he should not have many wives since if he does, they will cause idolatry to flourish, and he should not have many horses because if he does, he will be tempted to invade Egypt. But King Solomon feels quite confident that the law does not apply to him since he can have many wives and there will be no increased idolatry and many horses without there being any likelihood of his invading Egypt, and so he gets more wives and more horses and more idolatry and invades Egypt. The story is cited to warn us against treating the Torah as instrumental. If we view our religious obligations as having a reason and a purpose, we will immediately conclude that there is surely a better way to achieve the same end and the mitzvah will be abandoned. In recent years, many Jews concluded that the reason pork had been prohibited was to prevent Jews from getting trichinosis. But if the meat were cooked well enough they wouldn't get trichinosis anyway and so there were a lot of Jews who started eating pork.

Throughout the generations there have variously been those who have argued that our religious laws are reasonable and understandable, those who have held that only some of them can be explained, and those who have insisted that even if there are apparent explanations, they don't really count, the explanations are essentially irrelevant. The system can only be preserved if the tradition is observed for its own sake. Most of the time it all works pretty well and we don't have to choose up sides. Our inherited tradition is, on the face of it, sufficiently intelligible that many of us don't mind following it and in fact get pleasure out of doing so. At the same time, it is sufficiently obscure that we can't readily penetrate all of its categories for our convenience and understanding. Usually, it is a nice, but delicate balance, though we have to be careful not to let it tip too far to one side or the other. In the effort to keep that balance in place lies a very delicious religious struggle.

It is important that there be room in the Jewish community for Jews who say the old rules make no sense any longer, even in terms of the goals of traditional Jewish law. And there must also be room for those who hold that though the apparent reason no longer applies, the law does, that there is nothing perverse about Jews wanting to hallow a custom and add meaning to their lives by giving religious meaning not only to the meat they eat but the wine they drink as well.

If drinking bad wine is part of the price we have to pay for taking the Jewish tradition seriously, it isn't an outrageously high price. In fact, it is considerably less costly than many of our other Jewish commitments. But if on the other hand, we sometimes drink non-kosher Jewish wine, that may not lead us directly to idolatry, adultery, murder, and the total collapse of our Jewish lives. It is in the working out of such decisions as committed Jews that our tradition will be kept alive and well. L'haim! To life!

A Few Matters of Life and Death

Memorable Weddings

Some weddings are hard to forget.

It certainly was hard to forget a wedding I conducted in a fraternity house. At the end of the ceremony, when the groom stamped hard on the glass, the stuffed moose who had been balefully overlooking the entire event from above the mantle was jarred off the wall and crashed into the wedding cake and champagne.

But for sheer drama, that hardly compared to the time the other rabbi with whom I was co-officiating had a heart attack while we were signing the *Ketubah*, the marriage contract. An ambulance had to come and take him away. It took quite a while for that wedding to get started again, though not as long as the wedding at which the bride misplaced the civil license and my colleague, the other rabbi, wouldn't continue with the wedding until the license was recovered some five hours later, around midnight.

The rowdiest wedding I ever officiated at was one where the groom's mother punched out the bride's mother over a derogatory remark the bride's mother made about the father of the groom. People's nerves are often a little frayed at weddings.

Outdoor weddings can be very nice. Jewish tradition in fact recommends that weddings be conducted out-of-doors. The prettiest wedding site I have ever been at was in the middle of a state forest. The hardy wedding party drove into the woods as far as the rangers would allow and then in a high-heeled safari, trekked the wedding onto a high plateau.

The place the couple had selected for the _huppah_, the traditional wedding canopy, was a large flat rock overlooking an immense and beautiful meadow. But the altitude was so high that we had to deal with a brisk wind that turned the _huppah_ into a sort of parachute. After we tied the _huppah_ to the poles in order to keep it from flapping loose, there were moments when I was worried that the pole holders, one of whom was not very young, might be carried away over the cliff like four Mary Poppins holding bravely to their square, magic umbrella.

Even after the ceremony was over, the problems weren't all solved. They had planned to serve dozens of fancy little sandwiches at the reception but the toothpicks that were supposed to hold them together weren't sufficiently windproof. The tops kept blowing off until the serving people figured out that they could hold the sandwiches down by putting rocks on their lids. They tasted good once you brushed off the dirt.

Though I have officiated at many other outdoor weddings, one of the other special ones was when two dogs, apparently captivated by the romance of the occasion, began mating directly in front of the _huppah_. I got so rattled by the dogs that I forgot the names of the couple I was marrying. Though it happened at an outdoor wedding, now, even at indoor weddings, I always write down the names of the bride and groom on a little slip of paper and put it in my rabbi's book, even if I know them very well, just in case. I also keep my eye out for dogs.

Sometimes, people go out of their way to make weddings memorable. At one such wedding that comes to mind, the father of the bride was the president of a distinguished cooking school and had placed on exhibit a bas relief portrait of his daughter, carved in multi-colored cocoa butter.

A wedding that might have been memorable involved a couple that had met each other and me when we were all out running together. They wanted me to officiate at the end of a 10K road race with all of us dressed in our running shorts. I had heard of such weddings before (leaping out of airplanes, under water, on the backs of elephants, etc.) and agreed that it was a lovely sentimental idea, but it wasn't for me.

Trying to make a wedding memorable doesn't work. It only ends up being a little tacky. A truly memorable wedding has to just happen. It becomes memorable through its own internal energies.

In the course of conducting weddings over the years, I have come to a number of conclusions I should like to share. Perhaps they will be of assistance to people who are in the process of planning weddings. These are Israel's Laws of Weddings:

1. While wedding dates are often advanced, they are never deferred. A deferral is a prelude to a cancellation, even though the couple in question may not know it.

2. The number of guests increases exponentially with each additional category of friends or family.

3. It will cost minimally fifty percent more than you expect, whatever you expect.

4. A successful wedding is one in which you lose no more than two friends and three relatives.

5. A wedding without steady and clear direction is a vacuum which will immediately be filled by the florist, the band-leader, the caterer, Aunt Sarah or the rabbi. There is nothing wrong with that happening, but it will happen better if you decide in advance whose guidance is most likely to meet your needs.

6. The most important wedding law of them all: The things that go wrong at a wedding are what make it truly memorable. The things that go right evaporate into the past and become part of every other wedding that ever happened. But if the bride trips on her way down the aisle and falls flat on her face, if the groom gets caught in traffic and arrives very late, if the ring gets lost or the caterer serves ptomaine, everyone will remember the wedding warmly and chuckle about it for years. The disaster will have made the wedding.

It may only be a statistical accident but every one of the memorable weddings I have described here is still an intact marriage. Alas, that is something I cannot say about all the less eventful weddings in which I have participated.

The Talmud recounts that in the middle of a wedding, Mar, the son of Ravinah, picked up an extremely valuable cup and smashed it to bits. He certainly must have gotten everyone's attention because the incident caused that wedding to be remembered for about two thousand years. The reverberations from the breaking of that cup are heard when the glass is broken at every Jewish wedding, the broken glass that suggests that nothing is perfect, that every event and every moment is flawed, even those we treasure the most. Broken shards are among the givens of our lives. To forget that is to burden our legitimate aspirations with the pain of unnecessary disappointment.

It is an illusion to believe that you can be completely in control of anything in this world. So, as you plan your wedding, try to make it nice but don't try too hard. It isn't going to be perfect in any case. But even if you could create an extraordinary event that would be absolutely perfect, it would be so without character that no one would ever remember it.

Relax, enjoy and look forward with eager anticipation to the surprise mishaps that will make your wedding quite special and memorable. As for me, I still have two more children to marry off. When the time finally arrives, I wonder what will go wrong.

Washing the Dead

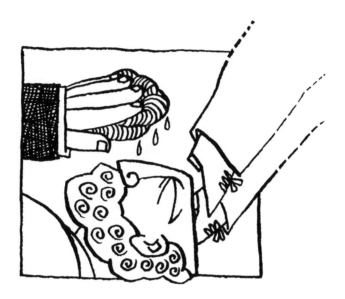

couldn't have anticipated that I would volunteer to wash the dead. I had never even *gone* to a funeral until I had to conduct one, a month after I finished rabbinic school. There was a mix-up. I eulogized the wrong person. Though the family never believed me, I swear it wasn't my fault. It was a terrible experience.

My first close encounter with a dead body was even worse. I was serving as a hospital chaplain at Bellevue. The office received a call from the emergency room saying that the police had just recovered a man from the East River. He had probably been there for about a month and it was no longer possible to tell whether he might have been Jewish, or for that matter anything else.

When an unidentified body arrived, the chaplains were called in one by one to administer appropriate religious rites. In Jewish tradition, there were no rites I could perform for the poor fellow. But since the hospital staff was mostly Catholic and pious, we didn't want to convey the notion that Jews didn't care about their dead. When called, the Jewish chaplains came too.

The nurse brought me in, pulled back the sheet, closed the door behind her and left me with the gruesome decaying body. I looked at it, concluded that the situation I was in was bizarre, and started to giggle. My giggle turned into hearty laughter. It was with great effort that I stifled the noise so that the nurses out in the hall wouldn't hear me.

When I did settle down, I began to feel guilty. How could I have laughed? What disrespect! I know now, though I didn't then, that the body was funny because I didn't know how to deal with my fear of the corpse.

With such a background, it is a continuing source of surprise to me that some of the more significant moments in my life as a Jew have come from my participation in the work of a local _Hevra Kadisha_, the Burial Society (literally, Holy Society). By now I can be in the presence of the dead without experiencing more fear or revulsion than I can control. That is not to say that being with the dead is always easy, but it does always seem important. I value the discomfort I still feel from time to time. I don't want to become hardened to death.

Readying the dead for burial is the only service we can perform for others in the absolute certainty they will never be able to reciprocate.

For that reason, the Jewish tradition holds that the task of washing and clothing bodies so that they are properly prepared to meet their Maker is particularly worthwhile.

The white linen pants, shirt, coat and hat that we use are much like the dress the Bible describes as appropriate for the High Priest on Yom Kippur, the Day of Atonement. Some say they are a simple festive costume, an approximation of what a well dressed Jew of the first century wore for special celebrations and important occasions. Either way, it is the right clothing to be dead in.

Mr. Gorelick, with whom I usually work, is in his early nineties. He is stooped and carries his head crooked to the side. Though he appears quite frail, experience has shown me that he is much tougher than I originally believed. I am convinced that he avoids a personal encounter with the Angel of Death because of their close professional relationship. They work together so comfortably, it is hard to imagine that either would want to dissolve the partnership. Mr. Gorelick is not morose or flippant as he goes about his work. He is respectful and quite matter of fact, humorless and businesslike.

Gorelick usually calls me at dinner time. "Can you come tonight? Any time is fine." If I don't have a prior commitment, I try to say yes. We usually start out at ten or eleven and finish up about midnight. The funeral home is all ours at night. The downstairs room in which we work has no clock or windows. Neither we nor the dead require them.

When the family of the dead requests it, there is one other person in the building, Goldfarb, the *shomer* or watchman, the man who is supposed to stay near the body until it is buried. Once, the task probably included a responsibility to chase away mice, but now he only has to recite Psalms. Gorelick tells me that one time he arrived and found Goldfarb sound asleep. He came in, washed a body and left and Goldfarb never woke up. "...And he claims to be a pious man," snorts Gorelick. "...And why does he say Psalms upstairs in the lounge? He should be with the body. He might as well say Psalms at home if he is going to stay upstairs."

Since traditional Jewish law prohibits embalming, these days the bodies are kept in a large refrigerator. "Mr. Gorelick," I argue, "the custom that the body should have a companion developed a long time ago. They didn't have refrigerators then. You can't expect Goldfarb to sit in the refrigerator all night. If he did that, we would be washing him." Gorelick mumbles something about Goldfarb and shakes his head.

The body is very carefully washed and then rinsed. The ritual takes place in silence. Watching hospital operations, I have always been unnerved by the casual chit-chat of the surgical teams. I understand that they cannot work well if they are under continual tension. Nevertheless, I am grateful that there is no talking during the washing of the dead. That makes it easier to remain aware of the significance of what we are doing.

After the washing, Gorelick puts some egg white mixed with a little vinegar on the closed eyes, under the nose, on the nipples and groin. I remember that it has to do with some complicated Kabbalistic doctrines of birth and death. I ask Gorelick if he can explain any of it to me. He can't. Feldblum, with whom I have worked occasionally, puts a little salt into the mixture. I ask Gorelick why Feldblum does it. Gorelick says, "Salt...it is nothing but foolishness and superstition...just like Feldblum to do that!"

Last year, Gorelick called me the night before Kol Nidre, the solemn evening which begins the fast of Yom Kippur. Would I come? I agreed to, even though it was a very hectic time for me. I felt sorry for the man who needed our services. It seemed a shame that he was not able to keep himself alive through Yom Kippur as so many others seem to. The nights just after Yom Kippur and Passover are unusually busy ones for the _Hevra Kadisha_. It is my private theory that the anticipation of Yom Kippur and the desire to achieve forgiveness helps people to hold on, while Passover, with all that food, does them in.

In the end, I was grateful for the call. My worship, that Yom Kippur, brought me into touch with my own mortality in ways that I rarely experience. When the recurring prayers asked "Who shall live and who shall die?"...this time, I really heard the questions.

The knee length coat tied with a linen belt, which is worn by the dead, is called a *kittel* ('little coat'). It is also customary among traditional Jews to wear a *kittel* during prayer on Yom Kippur. The kind of *kittel* that is worn on Yom Kippur is fancier than the *kittel* we use in the <u>H</u>evra Kadisha, but it is clearly the same garment. It is belted too, like the <u>H</u>evra Kadisha garment but it also has fasteners. It fastens "backwards," from a man's point of view, fasteners on the left, the opposite direction from most men's garments. The arrangement used on the *kittel* is also used on women's garments, which fasten in the same direction. The usual explanation is that it is presumed that someone else will help dress both women and the dead.

The knot we are required to use to tie the burial *kittel* belt is special. It is not very complicated, but I have never seen it used elsewhere. I tried to use the <u>H</u>evra Kadisha knot on my Yom Kippur *kittel*. It didn't work. It stays very tight on the dead, but doesn't seem to hold at all on the living. I do not know if this is intentional. No one I have asked has known. I speculate that if one of the bodies we had prepared for burial were to spring into life, surprised by the resurrection, we could be confident that the knots we had tied would not be encumbrances.

Once the body is dressed, we ask forgiveness of its former tenant in case we caused some indignity without intending to or behaved disrespectfully while we were preparing it for burial. It is presumed that the need to treat a person with decency does not cease with death. I recently read that the attorney general of one of the mid-Atlantic states gave permission to use unclaimed bodies to test automobile bumpers, not to test damage to the bodies, mind you, but damage to the bumpers.

I don't know if those bodies really cared, but the line between an offense to the living and an offense to the dead is so thin that the Jewish tradition has chosen not to acknowledge it.

After our work is finished, I am given fifteen dollars by the _Hevra Kadisha_. Happily, I don't need the fifteen dollars. Gorelick, I suspect, does. So does Mrs. Fein who washes the women. I learn that the women who work for the _Hevra Kadisha_ get only ten dollars. I am angry, having discovered that even here among the dead things are not fair. I complain to Gorelick and tell him that I won't come any more unless the women are paid the same as the men. He says it is all Feldblum's policy. It will be done right once he takes over from Feldblum. Later, when Gorelick has been put in charge, I ask Mrs. Fein what they are paying her. She won't tell me. I tell her why I want to know. She still won't tell me. I can't find out if she thinks it is none of my business or if Gorelick has gotten to her.

The _Hevra Kadisha_ in a nearby town sends the family of each person they prepare for burial an envelope containing a one hundred dollar bill and a note of explanation. The note encourages them to take the cash if they need it, no questions asked. On the other hand, if they can afford to, they should return the money and even add to it. In that way, the _Hevra Kadisha_ can provide for those who really are in need.

I suggest to Gorelick that this is something we should do. He says it would never work. We would go broke because the people we bury aren't as rich as the ones at the other _Hevra Kadisha_. Maybe Gorelick knows something I don't, but by the time they come to us, I can't see how anyone can tell who is rich and who isn't. No two look the same. It has to be the same at the other _Hevra Kadisha_. I think we should give it a try, but if Gorelick says no, it is no.

On previous nights, we had washed a sequence of rather stout men. They are hard to wash. It is only through being on the _Hevra Kadisha_ that I have come to understand what the term "dead weight" really means. Because of Gorelick's age, the heavy ones are particularly difficult for him. The grim reaper probably doesn't care much either way, but if one is to have compassion on the members of the <u>Hevra Kadisha</u>, it is well to approach the end svelte. The man we were washing this evening, however, who must have been in his late nineties, seemed to me almost weightless in comparison with those who had preceded him. He was nothing but skin and bones. I said so to Mr. Gorelick.

Gorelick was indignant. "What do you mean?" he said as we washed the corpse. "The man doesn't have cancer. There is no hint of arthritis in him. He isn't the least jaundiced. You're complaining? Why, this man is in terrific health!"

I had never really thought that being dead and healthy at the same time was one of the available options. It seemed to me that if you are dead, you are definitely not healthy. But this time, Gorelick was right.

Our bodies are ultimately rental property. They really belong to the Landlord of all the earth. Our relationships with our bodies ought to be that of responsible tenants who do their best not to ruin things. Though no tenant has an easy relationship with any landlord, if we are honorable, we won't do anything with the property that we wouldn't do in the presence of its owner. And when we have to vacate, it ought to be returned in the best possible condition. The man we were washing appeared to have achieved such an end.

I was only looking at the end of the man's life and Gorelick was looking at how he got there. What Gorelick realized and I forgot was that being dead is easy, while becoming dead well is a real trick. There are many ways to go, some better, some worse. Because Gorelick taught me, I now wish for myself, for Gorelick and for all of us, that when the time comes to go, may we go in the best of health.

The Spurious Kaddish

 had only been ordained a few months earlier. It was the first day of Rosh Ha-Shanah, the Jewish New Year, a new job and the first time I had ever preached to a really large congregation. The Torah scrolls had been put away and then it was time. I, the new rabbi, had to be

introduced to give the sermon. My boss, the senior rabbi, was to present me.

He was going to have a hard time. How can you introduce someone who has no experience, information or wisdom and tell a thousand people why they should be glad to have to sit and listen to him. Then I started to hear the introduction. That I worked well with students fit my own self-image. I liked that. When I learned that I was wise beyond my years, it tickled my vanity. But when I heard that I was a great Jewish scholar, then I knew that he must have been using a leftover introduction from an old file. And that was only the beginning. My saintliness and sagacity were detailed in ways that even my mother wouldn't have believed. I was becoming more embarrassed by the moment. Not only was he perpetrating a fraud, but a fraud that could not be concealed. The people sitting in front of me would know perfectly well immediately after I started speaking. He wasn't introducing me, he was giving my eulogy, and a fake eulogy at that. I don't know what I looked like but I felt as if I must have been red all over. I had to separate myself from that introduction, to let them know that they didn't have to believe it, because even I didn't believe it. What I really wanted to do was put the senior rabbi in as awkward position as he had put me, but I didn't think I could get away with it. Perhaps I could somehow extricate myself with some humor. Suddenly I remembered a great line I had heard someone else use in similar circumstances.

The Kaddish prayer is a doxology, a praise of God. It was originally said when one finished the study of sacred text, thanking God for that gift. Then, later on, it was said by analogy at the death of great scholars. Since time blurs all distinctions, the Kaddish finally came to be thought of as a prayer for the dead, whether scholars or not. I had been present a few weeks before when, prior to a lecture he was to give, a distinguished rabbi was introduced with a long and pompous introduction, the kind sometimes described as "epi-taffy." When the introduction was concluded the lecturer thanked the chairman for presenting him in such a generous way but in truth he felt that we should all rise for the Kaddish prayer for there was surely no live person who merited such praise. Everyone laughed.

When my florid introduction was finally completed and I came up to the pulpit, I knew I could help everyone to relax. "Now let us rise for the Kaddish," I said.

I waited for the chuckle so that I could proceed with my first High Holiday sermon. Unfortunately, there was more than a little wrong with my timing. To my horror, what I saw instead was the entire congregation, all thousand or so of them, rise for the Kaddish prayer. Never before or since have I been so flustered. Since they didn't understand what I had intended, could I actually ask them to say Kaddish with me? But it made no sense to say Kaddish at that point in the service. I couldn't tell them it was all a joke. If there had been anything even vaguely funny about my stunt, they wouldn't have been standing. I wanted a big fish to come by to swallow me up. I wanted to put on an invisible suit. I wanted to be somewhere else, someone else, I wanted it never to have happened. Anything.

I had heard of a new Ph.D. who was presenting his dissertation at the annual meeting of his professional association. When he was done, and it was time for the first question, someone got up and posed an extraordinarily difficult problem which cut the ground out from under all the work that he had done. The poor fellow fainted dead away on the spot. I wish I had been resourceful enough to faint.

What happened next? You are entitled to know that they aren't still standing there, but the details will have to wait for another time. It is still painful, after all these years. What I will tell you is that now, when someone introduces me, whether the introduction is simple or fancy, reasonable or outrageous, I say thank you and then I proceed with my speech. That's all. I try very hard not to be frivolous in serious situations. I do my best not to make light of rituals. I don't always succeed but I am much better than I was before this incident took place. The next time someone says Kaddish for me, it will be someone else. I said Kaddish for myself once. That was enough.

Bees and Jews

Being And Bee-ing

r. LaBrake was a real bee-keeper. He could sniff at the entrance to a hive and smell whether the colony had a queen. Once, when I had just gotten a couple of gratuitous stings, he glanced at the offending hive and said, "Of course you got stung, you darn fool. Just look at their flight pattern." I looked but I didn't see any flight pattern. All I could see were bees coming and going, the same as they did every other day. "Oh." I said. "Of course." I changed the subject and stayed away from the hives the rest of that day.

I am not a beekeeper. I just keep bees and have for the past twenty-five years. I grew up in a city and have lived all of my life in cities, but in one small corner of my imagination, utterly without justification, I fancy myself a country squire. My bees have helped foster that illusion. Growing basil and thyme in a kitchen flower pot doesn't achieve the same effect. Once I contacted City Hall and asked if I could keep chickens or a goat, but they said I could only keep chickens or a goat if I already had chickens or a goat. I might have pretended, but my neighbors have enough trouble with me now. They would never have let me get away with it. And so I make do with the bees.

Actually, my neighbors are at something of a disadvantage in dealing with my bees. Back in the middle of the nineteenth century, the Supreme Court declared that though they may be regulated, bees are definitionally beneficial to a community and therefore cannot be banned. (If the invasion of the Brazilian "killer" bees continues, this may change.) If my bee stings you, you can sue me, but first you have to prove it was my bee. Since bees die after they sting, it is a little hard to tell whether it was my bee that did the job. There are other bees in the neighborhood. I only own, or more accurately, provide housing, for a few of them.

I do my best not to be a bother to the neighbors. The problem tends to be my bees' drinking habits. When they are thirsty, they will go into wading pools, bird baths and hot tubs. No one has been stung yet, but some of the people nearby have been unnerved. It is very important for me to get them to use a water source in my own yard, first thing in the springtime. If I can get them accustomed to drinking at home, it is better for all of us. I also do my best to buy off the neighbors with jars of honey.

Depending upon the weather, my management skills, and various bee diseases like chalkbrood and American foulbrood and the Madagascar mite, I maintain two to five hives, including a glass-walled observation hive in the dining room. They yield from fifty to two hundred pounds of honey. We use a lot of the honey for cooking but we generally have more than we need. Because it seems too precious to sell, we give the rest away to friends and neighbors. Mr. LaBrake thinks that too is dumb.

Beekeeping in New England is (along with maple syruping) one of the last cottage industries still limping along. The people who do it cultivate a very folksy, down-home quality. At the beekeepers meetings they wear tie-pins with bees on them, work on embroidered bee cushions, serve honey-cherry pie or honey-sweetened tea. They also make a lot of bad puns. One of the companies advertises its equipment as Bee Ware. Another one signs all of its letters, "It's nice to bee with you." There is a journal called The Free Bee. At one of the national meetings, I opened the conference with an invocation which began "May we bee together in friendship and joy..." It was embarrassingly well received.

The beekeeping magazines are less distinctive. They are like every other hobby magazine, whether tropical fish breeding, photography, or dirt-bikes. They tell you about the latest equipment. They teach you about the latest technique. They attempt to inspire you to do it more. They give you biographical sketches about the people who do it best. And there are lots of ads. The bee magazines are only saved by the country flavor; a photo of the new Iowa Honey Queen, editorials about how young folks aren't taking to bees the way they did in the good old days and home remedies from the beehives.

Actually, the home remedies always amaze me. In other respects, beekeepers are down-to-earth practical people. But every year in the magazines there are new miracle cures from the bees. For a while, a mixture of honey and vinegar ("honegar") was certain to cure cancer. What is called royal jelly, a high protein substance the workers feed to the queen larvae, is held to add years to your life and life to your years. That is probably true if you are a queen bee but rather dubious if you are a person. Then the Danes began writing about the virtues of bee pollen to prevent impotence. Long-distance runners were using pollen for running endurance. Carefully placed bee stings are still touted as a cure for arthritis (in spite of all the arthritic and often stung beekeepers we all know from our beekeepers' society), and of course, there are always praises to the healthful benefits of honey in general, and in particular in the control of hay-fever and allergies. The list of cures is much longer but I personally don't believe in any of them.

Honey is a sugar. It is a sugar with a large percentage of fructose, an easily digestible sugar (found in an even greater percentage in fruit) but a sugar nonetheless. It is true that there are more trace minerals in honey than one would be likely to get in refined cane-sugar, but there is no reason the minerals found in honey should be preferred to those we get in ordinary fruits and vegetables and which can be ingested without eating all that sugar. I suppose it is not loyal of me to say it, but there is only one reason I know for eating honey. It tastes very good, particularly on ice cream. I think that is a fine reason and that it is silly to invent reasons to prove that it is especially good for you.

If the only honey you eat comes from the large honey-co-ops in the Midwest, you may not even know how good honey tastes. Honey is in some ways rather like maple syrup. It is processed plant nectar, whose water content is evaporated off until the viscous syrup remains. The extra fluid is removed from maple syrup by cooking and removed from honey through the fanning of bee wings. When honey reaches the right viscosity, the bees seal off the honey combs. At harvest time the large scale commercial beekeepers take all the honey from hundreds or even thousands of hives that may be distributed over a sizable area, not paying any attention to whether all of the cells are sealed or if some of them are not yet ripe enough for harvesting. Since unripe honey has a potential for spoiling, the large producers pasteurize all their honey, so that bacteria that could otherwise grow are destroyed. The cooking and filtering done by the big processors produces honey that is clear and sterile, but not usually very good tasting.

With honey, the less you do to it, the better it is. So I recommend you get your honey from a place like "Joe's Apiary". Joe, who may run a bicycle shop or a farm stand on the side, has so few hives that he can afford to take honey when it is ripe and leave it in the hive if it is not. He can go back another time and get it when it is ready. Furthermore, he probably cannot afford a lot of fancy processing equipment. As a result, his honey is usually much more tasty. Since ripe honey kept in a closed container at room temperature will never spoil, it just as safe as what you can buy in the supermarket.

I am continuously surprised about how much people want to know about bees. Rare is the party in which I have not been drawn into a conversation about them. I can't say that I am actually dragged into these discussions screaming, but I don't think I am usually the one to start them.

It used to be conventional wisdom that the three subjects people liked most to read about most were Abraham Lincoln, doctors and dogs. The perfect candidate for a best-seller, therefore, would be a book about Lincoln's doctor's dog. I think that list is wrong, or at least should be supplemented. Any list of most popular subjects has to include bees. Rare is the Sunday Magazine without an article about bees. The new reports on the northward progress of the Brazilian "killer" bees appears in the *New York Times* with predictable regularity. A swarm of bees in some unlikely place is always good for a photo on the front page of everyone's hometown newspaper. And every year there is a new popular book on the subject of bees. And so, if Lincoln's doctor's dog is still the preferred subject, if the dog, the doctor, or Lincoln were attacked by killer bees, the book simply couldn't miss.

It is not because they fear bees that people want to know about them. People fear wasps too, but they generally don't ask me that much about wasps. It is the communal structure of the bees that fascinates. They don't look like us, they don't act like us, but they have a complex society that appears to have many parallels to ours. It is this aspect of the life of the bee that has engaged writers for thousands of years. The behavior of the bee is used as a model for human behavior we want to justify and explain. It is comforting to think that our own conduct is as much a part of the natural order as is the bee's.

In Roman times, Pliny the Elder discusses not the queen bee but rather, the emperor bee. Since an emperor ruled Pliny's community, it was perfectly logical to him and the people of his time that a bee emperor would rule bees. In the time of the French monarchy, since they didn't have an emperor, French beekeepers wrote about the king bee. They took special interest in the phenomenon of succession in the hive. If the "king bee" is weak and not able to perform "his" tasks in the governance of the hive, a vigorous new "king" will be hatched who will emerge to duel with the old one and kill it. The French beekeepers note that worker bees never sting the royal bee, even if there might be good reason to do so. That is left for another royal bee to do. Good monarchists, those bees!

In 1609, six years after the death of Queen Elizabeth, an English beekeeper named Butler learned that the hive has a queen, not a king. Butler knew that a female was an effective ruler of his own society, so he could imagine a female presiding over a society of bees. His vision of human society appears to have conditioned what he was able to discover about the insect world.

I have seen Soviet beekeeping literature which, like the French, is very interested in the problem of succession. When a new queen is about hatch in the hive, the old queen, if she is permitted to do so, will go over to the new queen's cell and destroy her rival before she emerges. What especially intrigued Stalinist beekeepers was that if the old queen is infirm and no longer laying well, when a new queen is hatched, the workers prevent the young queen from being killed in her cell. The old queen is kept away until the rival emerges from her cell and duels with the presiding queen, usually killing her. To those old fashioned Marxists, the conclusion to be drawn is that the major decisions in the hive are not made by the queen, but rather by the workers, and the beehive is ultimately a Socialist society.

No-nonsense American beekeeping literature will often reject such anthropomorphizing of bees altogether. The hive does not have a "queen." That suggests personalty. It has an egg-laying mechanism, and if adequate supplies and environmental conditions are maintained, a maximum about of honey will be produced. Or as it was put it in the title of an article in *The Connecticut Honey Bee*, "Bees Run Efficient Factories." One can draw a similar conclusion from the title of an article about bees that recently appeared in the *Wall Street Journal*, "Queen Bee as CEO."

If everyone else does it, so can I. I should like to turn to a consideration of beekeeping in the Jewish tradition. That is probably not a subject that immediately leaps to your mind as you think about bees and I must warn you that it may be even less obvious than you think that bees and Jews have much to do with each other.

Middle eastern beekeeping precedes Jewish history by many years. Four to five thousand years ago, Egyptian beekeepers put their hives on rafts or barges at the headwaters of the Nile and floated them downstream toward the Mediterranean. As they travelled, they let their bees gather nectar along the banks of the Nile. When the beekeepers got to the end of the river, they sold their honey and took their barges back to start all over again.

But though there was beekeeping in the general area, there are no references to beekeeping in the Jewish literature of the period. The Bible knows about bees, but not about domesticating them. Furthermore, contrary to our own generally positive image of bees, all Biblical references to bees are negative. "The Amorites shall chase you like bees" (Deuteronomy 1:44) or, in reference to Israel's enemies: "The nations...have surrounded me like bees" (Psalm 118:2). The prophetess Deborah's name means bee, but she was less likely to be called that because she gathered sweets than because she had a sting as a warrior. The message was clear: bees were dangerous. Stay away from them. If you want to learn from the social insects as other peoples have, don't do it from bees. "Go, you sluggard, to the ant and consider her ways and be wise" (Proverbs 6:6).

The bees that are referred to in the Bible do not sound like the kind of honey bees we know. Our honey bees make their homes in trees, not rocks (Psalm 81:17). Samson's story (Judges 14) helps resolve some of the confusion. Samson goes to Timnah and on his way, kills a lion. When he returns, he sees its carcass and notices that inside it is a nest of bees. Samson then takes the bees' honey out of the carcass. The story points to a bee we do know today, namely the Syrian bee, which does put its nest in carcasses and in the ground, but which is rarely cultivated as a honey producer because it is mean, aggressive and not especially productive. Thus, the heroism of Samson is twofold: He killed a fierce lion and was able to get honey from those nasty bees.

The changes in the character of the references to bees and bee-keeping come with Roman contacts with the Land of Israel. Even though the Roman conquest was cruel, the Romans did bring with them those gentle Italian honey bees we use to this day. Western civilization's literary image of the bee is to be credited to the Italian variety. Although it must be treated with respect, the Italian bee is not mean.

These different strains of bees account for the different attitudes to the bee in the Jewish Bible and in the Roman Church. In Church literature, the bee becomes a symbol of the productive, self-sacrificing virgin. That is why the bee is displayed on the Pope's miter, a kind of theological bee in the bonnet. That image of the bee didn't work at all for ancient Jews, since every time they got near one of those Syrian virgins in the Holy Land, they got badly stung.

After the Roman conquest, the Jewish attitude to bees changes. Rabbinic literature begins to discuss systematic beekeeping, controlling of swarms and the crushing of combs to remove honey (an almost universal practice until the middle of the nineteenth century). The size of hives and the materials they were made of are described in the Talmud: clay cylinders made of earth and chopped straw, about forty inches high and ten across; hives very similar to those many Arabs use to this day. One finds Talmudic references to the medicinal effects of honey. When applied to wounds, it in fact has a powerful bactericidal effect because it is both acid and viscous, with strong osmotic power, desiccating any bacterium unlucky enough to find its way into it.

But as tasty and useful as it was, honey presented a problem for the rabbis. Bees don't chew the cud or have split hooves. In the Talmud, they fall into the taxonomic category of unclean birds. Observant Jews, who eat neither unclean animals nor the products of unclean animals, are therefore presented with the problem of whether they are permitted to eat honey. If you don't eat pork, neither do you drink pig milk. If you don't eat ostrich, you don't eat ostrich eggs. Since we don't eat bugs, how then can we eat a bug product, honey?

The rabbis argue the question in the Talmud. There are those who thought that we need not worry because the bees do not make honey, they are merely syrup collectors who go from flower to flower collecting sweet syrup for their little buckets (Bekhorot 7b). Sorry, the bees do process the honey; what goes into the bee is not what comes out of the bee. Besides, when you eat honey, no matter how carefully you process it, little parts of the bee find their way into the honey. How then is it not the product of an unclean animal, or even an unclean animal itself? Why may we eat it?

Even though all of the fancy legal arguments show why honey is prohibited, observant Jews are permitted to eat it for some very straightforward common sense reasons. Because we have been eating it for years and if there had been anything really wrong with it, someone would have said so long ago. And besides, how could any kind of honey have been a prohibited food? God couldn't have promised us a land flowing with milk and honey and then told us not to eat it.

Honey is in many respects an extraordinary food. One pound of honey is the lifes' work of about nine hundred bees. They have had to fly a distance which is equivalent to many times around the world in order to gather it. Experiencing that fact makes it impossible for me to deal casually with my honey. It is not an exaggeration to say that I find it a holy product.

But what for me is most unusual about it is not the honey itself, but the way the bees function in order to produce it. A modern beehive takes the form of a number of wooden boxes set on top of each other. In each of the boxes there are usually ten sheets of wax on wooden frames. On these, the bees raise their young and store honey. The bees form themselves into a round cluster on the frames so that there is a ball of bees inside a cube of hive. On the outer edges of the hive, the bees store honey, closer to the center, they store pollen, and in the middle, where it is warmest and most protected, they place their young. That means that a single frame taken out of the side of the hive will contain mostly honey, while one taken from the center will be mostly young bees about to hatch.

Bees allocate tasks within the hive on the basis of their age. The youngest serve as nurse bees to larvae that need tending. The oldest bees are field foragers who go out to seek nectar. If, as I do once a year, I take a single frame out of a large hive and put it into my glass-walled one-frame observation hive, most of the bees on the frame will have been doing their specialized, age specific tasks. Nevertheless, within minutes of taking out the frame, all the bees redistribute their tasks so that every one of the jobs necessary to the hive is still being performed. They have overridden their biological programming and reorganized themselves quickly, efficiently, peacefully and without apparent discussion or even a vote. No one knows how that happens.

In discussing bread, Rabbi Ben Zoma is quoted in the Talmud as saying: "What an enormous amount of work Adam, the first man, had to do before he found a crust of bread to eat. He had to plow and sow, reap and bind sheaves, and thresh and winnow, and sift and bake and only afterwards, he ate. And I get up in the morning and eat" (Berakhot 58a). It is not only the interrelatedness of the many facets of the natural world that puts bread on our plates in the morning, but also the interrelatedness of people. That is probably why bread is considered by the

Jewish tradition to be the quintessential food and always worthy of blessing.

As bread is the miracle produced by an unruly human community, often not given to cooperative ventures, honey is to me the miracle produced by the cooperative activity of a big box of bugs. It is quite astonishing. That is why I feel perfectly comfortable looking at my hives and saying the benediction the Jewish liturgy requires be said when one has experienced the wondrous. "Blessed are You, O God who has performed a miracle for me at this place."

Jews and Wasps: Cultures in Conflict

Or
The Unwelcome Guests Of Sukkot

B y now, just about everyone who knows I keep bees has asked me if I have heard the one about why honeybees wear yarmulkes, traditional skullcaps. The answer is: So that no one should think they are wasps.

The joke isn't particularly funny, and bees do not have little black caps. Still, I must admit I have some fondness for the joke no matter how many times I am forced to pretend I have never heard it before.

I am pleased to have whatever support is available from that rather small portion of the world's population that believes one ought to distinguish between bees and wasps, particularly at the time of Sukkot.

Pressed by assimilation and anti-Semitism, Jews have never had an easy time of it. But one sharply pointed problem of Jewish life that has almost always been ignored is the recurring trouble that comes from wasps, not bees, in the sukkah. The fact is that bees and wasps are not the same and there is too much bad-mouthing of bees by people who can't tell the difference. I am weary of phone calls from neighbors who swear they have just been attacked by my bees. I have to go over to their houses and yards and get rid of their wasp nests in order to mollify them. Often Jews don't seem very tuned in on what's going on out there in the natural world.

Two tailors decided to be adventurous. Instead of going to Miami for vacation as they usually did, they signed up for an African safari. They were deep in the jungle when they heard an enormous roar just behind them and went straight up the nearest tree barely ahead of a very large and hungry looking beast. "What is it?" asked one. Answered the other, "I should know? You think I am a furrier?"

The interest in taxonomy shown by those two tailors is not very different from that generally seen in most Jews I know who eat their meals in the sukkah. In the hope of sophisticating some Jewish sensibilities, I should like to try to make a few distinctions.

The first rule of thumb is, if they are bothering you late in the springtime, they are probably bees. If they are bothering you in the fall, they are more likely to be wasps.

Honey bees are fuzzy. Wasps are smooth. Bees are stocky around the waist. (No hips on a real bee.) Wasps on the other hand have skinny "wasp waists." Both are yellow and black, but bees are slightly more orange colored. The Italian honey bees we generally see around our yards (no, they are not killer bees) have three black bands on their tails. Bees eat only sweet things. Wasps can be interested in sweets but they like meats and fats even more.

There are many more differences but they are probably not relevant. It is hard to concentrate on details like wing shape and size (once again, long and thin on the wasps) when whatever it is, is buzzing around your nose. And when it is finally quiet because it is dead, it doesn't much matter what it used to be. But in the fall, at the time of Sukkot, you ought to assume that you are probably dealing with wasps. The drier the fall weather is, the more they seem to be on the prowl.

You may have paper wasps...a kind of wasp that makes a hanging, gray, football-shaped nest. Bee hives are always inside something like a tree or a house. If you are certain that they are out to get you, because they have built their nest right over your doorway or in your front bushes and attack you every time you come in the house, you should probably kill them. Spray them with wasp spray, a powerful jet of insecticide that can be applied from a safe distance at night when they are all at home and can't easily find you to attack. But if they are attached under some distant set of eaves and you would have to climb a precarious ladder to get near, forget about them. The cure is more dangerous than the malady. The colony will be dead by spring and will not be reinhabited. The chances are that there are many more wasps in the neighborhood than can be accounted for by that one nest. If you destroy it you are not likely to experience a big difference.

Wasps aren't all bad. There have been those who raised the tough question of why The One Who is All Wise created mosquitoes. Since there appears to be no better or more straightforward explanation, and unaware of ecological niches, some teachers were forced to conclude that it must be that it was in order to test the mettle of the people of Israel. In the case of wasps there is a somewhat less theologically demanding answer.

You may be one of the people who comes from the sort of authentic Jewish home in which the difference between spiders and cockroaches is considered philosophy. If that is your background, discriminating among bees and wasps is probably not a high priority issue. Nevertheless, you should know that the world would be a poorer place and we more miserable without wasps. We owe them no small debt of gratitude for the large quantities of very unpleasant bug larvae they eat. They are quite useful in holding down the insect population. However, that bit of wisdom never seems to console anyone very much at lunchtime during the festival of Sukkot.

Based on the latest entomological information available, I should like to suggest that those of you who take meals in a sukkah have a number of alternatives to consider (none of them very good) as you attempt to deal with wasps.

Jewish law insists that we try to establish a truce between ourselves and the animal kingdom on our sacred days. This means no trapping or killing, including the trapping or killing of bugs. When the legal material gets down to actual cases, dangerous beasties like scorpions don't get much protection while bothersome ones like fleas get some (*Shulhan Arukh, Orekh Haim: Hilkhot Shabbat*, 397). Since it was not clear to me as to where wasps fell on the dangerous-bug list, in the hope that I could reduce the wasp population of my sukkah, I bought some commercial wasp traps and hung them, pretending they were mere sukkah decorations. It was a sensational idea. I had fantasies of making a real killing and selling wasp traps by the dozen in all the local synagogues. All I succeeded in catching were a couple of house flies.

Among the more desperate measures taken by one of my friends is a bait-and-switch technique. A splendid plate of food is placed outside of the sukkah so that the wasps can eat the decoy food and ignore what is on the inside. Unfortunately, the wasps never seem to know which plate is intended specially for them. They just divide up forces and enjoy. There are always more than enough wasps around for the plates in both places.

Another such quixotic technique (same friend) is known as "spray-the-s'hakh," the thatching on the sukkah roof. That works very well to keep the wasps off the s'hakh, just not off your lunch...unless of course you spray sufficiently to have wasp spray wafting through the air of the sukkah, poisoning you and your wasps simultaneously.

You can pray for snow. If your prayers are answered, this one works very well. They never have wasps in the sukkot of Siberia. Though wasps can fly about in colder temperatures than bees, they can't fly when the temperature really drops. Wasps don't come into the sukkah during the rain either, but then neither do people.

During the day-time, get in and out of your sukkah as fast as you can and don't put out food that the wasps might like, until the instant you sit down. It won't take them a long time to find your cholent, that delicious meaty dish, but you can get at least a small lead on them.

Clean up fatty trash, meat and sweets after your meal so that the wasps won't get used to hanging around continuously. Since they can't navigate in the dark, eat your major and leisurely meal at night when the wasps are sleeping-in.

Some people may want to consider serving Pritikin type menus, meals devoid of sugars and fats. The down-side is that not only are the wasps unlikely to be very interested in this kind of food, your family isn't likely to want it either.

There are a few situations in which ordinary bees and wasps will attack without apparent provocation. That can happen if they feel their nests are endangered. You may not have noticed that you were near one until it was too late. Sometimes too they will become quite irritable from the fumes just after a gas mower has finished a lawn.

Because, unlike bees, they do not die after they sting, wasps are far more profligate about stinging at such times than are bees. Wasp stingers are smooth and not left behind after they have stung (...another clue as to what it was that stung you). When bees sting, they generally lose their barbed stingers and their poison sacs in your flesh. That is why the rarer bee stings are generally more virulent than the hit-and-run stings of the wasps who keep their equipment intact.

Unless you are trying to get away from a nest, it makes no sense to try to run away from them or shoo them away. They are much faster than you. There is no way to escape if they really want to get you. But except in the special circumstance I have described, neither bees nor wasps are really interested in you. They want your food. So if you are sitting in your sukkah or in the yard and don't try to sit on, play with or eat the wasps, as near as they get and as bothersome as they can be, they will generally not actually attack you. The folks who get stung have usually swatted them first. Don't swat!

It is very hard to convince someone who is genuinely afraid, but even if wasps are sitting on your fork full of food or drinking from a glass of sweet juice or wine that you are about to put to your lips, if you continue going about your business and eat in a reasonably ordinary way without too many jerky motions...and you don't need to go into slow motion...they will be gone before you get too close. If you stay casual, they will stay casual. They will fly away as if they never noticed you were in the vicinity, though in fact you may have been within three or four inches of their little black feet.

Our lives are generally rather well modulated. We go from heated and cooled homes to heated and cooled cars. We go up and down in elevators and walk only if essential. We do our best even to play only in carefully controlled environments. The festival of Sukkot urges us to not to delude ourselves. We are entitled to security but must not lose sight of our vulnerability. Though a properly constructed sukkah provides shelter, it must be open to the sight of the sky. At the season of harvest and plenty the sukkah directs our attention to the evanescent quality of all life, the blessing of rain and growth, and the curse of want.

There is a world out there with an agenda that often does not correspond with ours and that does not routinely adjust itself to our needs. It has a majesty and a reality of its own that we in our comfort sometimes ignore. The wasps, those uninvited and unwelcome guests with whom we reluctantly share our sukkot, are very useful messengers to remind us of the holiday theme, that the earth and its fullness is God's and that we are all guests in the sukkah.

Running Torah

Judaism and Jogging
Or
The Rambam Wore Sweats

I am an obsessive jogger. I take great pride in the number of years that go by without my missing a day. (Eighteen, at this writing.) Though a tornado might give me pause, thus far bad weather has never kept me from running. Boston's famous blizzard of '78 was for me a delightful occasion to run on the streets without having to worry about traffic.

My big achievement was discovering how to run on Jewish fast days. When a fast is just over and everyone else is busy eating, I go out and break my fast with a quick run of a few miles. I find that it peps me up far more than the food I take later.

I am almost never ill now that I am running, and when I am, I am likely to lie about it. On the rare occasions that I actually have a fever, I run fewer miles, run after my sensible wife is out of the house, but run nevertheless.

If an airplane trip keeps me from running in the morning, I become irritable and begin to manifest clear withdrawal symptoms. As one who is mainlining running, it is difficult for me to function until I get my fix. I am not as obsessive as some of my friends who jog in place in airplane washrooms, but still, I am a trifle possessed. I divide the year into two segments, preparation for the Boston Marathon and recovery from it.

I am certainly not a competitive runner. My finishing position will never be within a zip code of one of the official winner's places. For three consecutive years I ran the Boston Marathon five minutes faster each year and each of the three years I lost an additional thousand places. Discouraging, but not discouraging enough to keep me from con-tinuing to run the Marathon.

Running is for me physical fitness, weight control, meditation, thanksgiving, psychotherapy, thinking time and personal challenge. I believe it to be the magic elixir which can cure everything but baldness and if I am to be really candid, I even have a few hidden hopes about that.

Running is also a cause of embarrassment. It is something a proper rabbi ought not do. And so, when I run by my local synagogue, some people are amused, some are faintly uncomfortable and look at me disapprovingly and a few have decided that I am not there. The latter group and I have a tacit agreement that if I am wearing my running suit I can't see them and they can't see me. When I put on my clothes and slow to a walk, our vision is miraculously restored.

What is wrong with running? Why is it that some very nice Jews view the whole thing as at best silly and at worst a clear manifestation of a lack of piety? I could always point out that the introduction to the *Shulhan Arukh*, the classic code of Jewish law, that says one should run like a deer in the service of God. Consider Psalm 119:32: "I will run to do your commandments, for you will enlarge my heart." Doesn't that sound as if God knows that aerobic exercise is good for the cardiovascular system? In fact we all know that the text doesn't really mean it and that running receives about as much attention in classic Jewish sources as is given to discussion of color TV reception in pre-Israelite Jericho.

But if nothing in the literature supports running, neither can I find any clear prohibitions against it. To be sure, there are some who would consider normative running attire a bit immodest, bare legs showing and all. On the Shabbat, one is only supposed to run rapidly in the direction of the synagogue, but should go slowly leaving it. I know of only few people who consider that more than a sweet sentiment.

But if there are no negative references to running in particular, there are in the tradition many negative attitudes to athletics and athletes.

Resh Lakish, the athletic Talmudic master, once earned his living as a kind of circus gladiator. The moment he decided to devote his life to the study of Torah, he became too weak to put his armor back on. Starting with Samson, there are almost no favorable comments about men of strength. Only non-Jews are robust, and so we find the Yiddish saying that someone is *gesunt vie a goy*, as healthy as a non-Jew. In Eastern Europe, the strongest man in the *shtetl*, the Jewish village, was

the wagon driver, who was at the bottom of the
most prestigious figure, the yeshivah scholar wh
academy, was generally skinny, pale and w
enough to carry the volumes of Talmud he was

In addition to the question of exercise, ther
Jewish cultural heritage that discourages exerc
is that we come from a culture in which depri
sufficiency the exception. Corpulence, theref
success, skinniness a measure of failure. Even
yeshivah student, you knew that if you studiec
ried off to a rich man's daughter and they v
enough. In such a culture you eat all you can
Jewish mother's dream was to have a plump c

This theme still plays itself out today. It is
wedding like the sort of non-Jewish wedding
ber sandwiches and petit fours and have a
and Italian weddings are like most Jewish v
came from cultures of poverty in which th
excess of food.)

Today, in our culture of affluence, every
feast. Unfortunately, our bodies function und
that every feast will be followed by famine an
calorie we take in and slow down our metab
diet. We eat like lumberjacks and burn off calc

Jewish tradition is not indifferent to q
discussions almost invariably concern them
we should eat, the intake and output of bo
ness—but never with exercise, cholesterol o

If you work in the fields and spend m
hard physical labor, you don't need addit

probab
you do
It i
what w
by pro
yeshiva
great ir
needed
were n
port fro
the issu
Mos
Hutchir
would li
heart at
very go
lent rab
person.
believe i
I bla
Clas:
culture.
resented
an abom
gral part
technolo
Greek cu
tion rem
and on t
athletic g

y get by without worrying about how much you eat, but what if
't do physical work?

said that the late Rabbi Abraham Isaac Kook, first chief rabbi of
s then Palestine, tried to change the Jewish attitude to exercise
osing calisthenics as part of the curriculum for his inactive
1 students. He believed that the world was about to receive a
fusion of spiritual force and to be able to receive it well, we
to cultivate strong bodies. Kook failed. His recommendations
ver followed. In spite of his great prestige, he received no sup-
n the rest of the rabbinic community and ultimately dropped
.

of my rabbinic peers are forever quoting me Robert Maynard
s famous adage that whenever he got the urge to exercise, he
down and wait until it passed over. When Hutchins died of a
ack before his time, a number of years ago, he didn't make a
d case for his views, though his demise didn't make any indo-
s I know start to exercise. It is harder to kill an attitude than a
nd so the question remains, why don't most traditional Jews
running or any other form of exercise?

ne it on the Greeks.

ical Judaism was very ambivalent about the Greeks and their
he political intrusions of the Alexandrian empire were deeply
The attempts to make Jews serve Greek gods were considered
nation, but all the while, Greek culture was becoming an inte-
of the Jewish world; Greek trade, Greek vocabulary and Greek
y entered the life of the Jewish community. Some aspects of
ture seemed morally neutral. About these, the rabbinic tradi-
ined silent. Others were in direct conflict with Jewish values,
ese the rabbis took a stand. One of those rejected areas was
mes.

It would be a mistake to assume that the term game implied a measure of play for the Greeks. To the contrary, the games were a very serious business. Greeks didn't exercise. Physical fitness for its own sake would have seemed like a frivolous activity. They had no interest whatever in a regimen of physical activity which did not lead directly to increased proficiency, either as warriors or as athletic contestants, and the distinction between the two was not very great.

The games were originally an opportunity for soldiers to demonstrate military skills, and later became para-military training for young men who might be called upon to defend their cities. Among the Greek cities, it was only Sparta that did not have an active gymnasium program, and that was because all of their young men were always in military camps. They didn't need to be trained for the reserves since they were already in the regular army.

The root of the term "athletics" means prize, and winning was an athlete's sole goal. Greek athletic games were not "sports." They implied no concept of sportsmanship. There was no value attached to doing one's best, no notion of coming in a close second. There was only one issue, winning. All else was disgrace. No silver or bronze medals were given to the also-rans. The man who came in second was just one of many losers.

Since the games were confrontations and not sports contests, there was nothing considered wrong with maiming or killing an opponent. Death was not such a bad outcome for a loser. It didn't earn him a hero's burial, but in dying, he could salvage a few scraps of honor even though he had lost.

Athletics, like everything else supported by the state, was intimately tied up with Greek religion. It was impossible to participate in the games without paying one's respects to the gods of the Greek pantheon. Today's ritual of carrying the Olympic torch is a vestigial relic of the

Greek torch races in which fire was brought from one god's sacred altar to another. Since Greek religion had far less to do with sin and good deeds than it did with triumph and failure, gods were asked for victory before the games, and thanked with offerings for success after them. Gods were also invoked as the guarantors of the rules established by the judges. There are reports of Jewish athletes who tried to join the games without deferring to the gods, but their attempts were clearly a rarity and do not seem to have met with any great measure of success.

Gymnasium means a place of nakedness. Within the gymnasium there was a considerable amount of sexual activity. Heterosexuality was, to the classical Greek mind, a moderately dull option available to any run-of-the-mill animal. Homosexuality was the uniquely human act, the bit of culture and civilization that could be added to ordinary sex. The central activity of the gymnasium was the transmitting of manly skills to young men through the guidance and advice of older experienced men, none of them wearing any clothes. Within this context, erotic relationship between adolescents and middle-aged men developed routinely. Pederasty was a commonplace feature of the gymnasium.

The Greeks were not very interested in what went on inside the body, but they were enthralled with its external aesthetics. A well-proportioned, muscular body was appreciated as a thing of great beauty. Greek poetry, pottery and sculpture pay greatest attention to the athletes and sports where muscular, well developed bodies were most likely to be found. The Greeks had no use for the emaciated look of the long-distance runner. A measure of Greek disinterest in long-distance running is the fact that the longer the race, the smaller the prize the winner received. The longest of the Greek foot races was about three miles. The story of Pheidippides, dropping dead as he did after delivering the good news from Marathon to Athens certainly showed that the Greeks didn't do much long-distance training. That story also gave long distance running a bad name for a long time after. The Marathon as a race is a modern invention.

It is not hard to see why the rabbis of the Talmud didn't think much of athletes or athletics.

The rather non-militaristic traditions of rabbinic Judaism could have had little use for a set of activities glorifying the military. A religion in which male homosexuality, frequently associated with pagan rites, was to be punished with death would have been unenthusiastic about a setting in which homosexuality was looked upon as a higher form of culture. A tradition in which proper conduct is judged far more important than outcome could not easily have accepted activities in which outcome is everything. A tradition which viewed the body as a receptacle for the divine spirit could not value one in which the body is glorified for its own sake.

An enterprise which led Jewish young men to attempt to surgically conceal their circumcisions so that they could participate in athletics without self-consciousness alongside the Greeks could not have been thought to be good for the Jews. No matter how charitably one judged the enterprise, if it caused Jews to try to break their covenant with God, it had to be viewed with alarm.

Antiochus the Fourth, the despised Syrian king of the Hanukkah story, was an enthusiast of Greek culture. In a unique appointment, he was made president of the Olympic games. It is not surprising that one of the events which lead to the outbreak of the Maccabean revolt was his attempt to establish a gymnasium in Jerusalem. To the Jews, the gymnasium and athletics represented the worst in heathen culture.

The distance between Jews and athletics became even greater in Roman times than it had been during the Greek period. Athletic games were symbolized at that time by the fights of gladiators in which the deaths of some of the combatants was not only possible, as it had been in the Greek games, but certain, and some of those required to fight were captured Jews.

It is still a live memory. An article in the *Jerusalem Post* (U.S. Edition, May 27-June 2, 1979), entitled "Stadium Attacked as 'Pagan,'" describes a demonstration by tens of thousands of religious Jews. It goes on to say "...the Chief Rabbinate Council called on the mayor to cancel the stadium project 'because it would imbue Jerusalem with Hellenistic culture, a spirit which our forefathers fought against throughout history.'"

In the middle ages, there appears to have been some Jewish athletic activity from time to time—fencing, horseback riding, and mock jousts at weddings—but it never received much rabbinic encouragement. The basic stance had already been taken. It is hard to develop much of an interest in physical sports in a tradition which claims that one of the reasons the Temple was destroyed was that Jews played ball on Shabbat. (Lamentations Rabbah 2:4) For close to a thousand years, the major Jewish athletic endeavor has been chess.

Once, we lived under the illusion that Israelis would change the old image; that they would become Jewish models of health and strength. It didn't work. American Jews are far more health and fitness conscious than Israelis. Israeli men live with the illusion that because they were once in the Israeli army and continue to serve in the reserves, they are tough and fit, regardless of the reality that overtakes them in subsequent years when they overeat and do not exercise.

Thus it is the rabbinic tradition which we must still confront if we are to develop a Jewish ideology for exercise.

I have no major quarrel with the rabbis' rejection of Greek athletics. Furthermore, some of the issues that bothered them are still relevant. I think it is very difficult for Jewish law to justify the violence involved in professional football, boxing or hockey. Nevertheless, the rabbinic rejection of athletics should not remain with us as a blanket rejection of all athletic activity, as it presently seems to be. I should like to argue that running and probably a fair number of other sports are different.

There are three different kinds of legitimate satisfaction that can be derived from exercises like running: health, pleasure, and challenge. None of them require the harming of people, the mutilation of one's own, or anyone else's body. Runners, cyclists or swimmers may pull tendons or have sore knees, but such injuries they experience are more likely to be from a lack of good judgment than an excess of heroism. They are not the inevitable consequence of the sport.

In the sport I know best, most runners don't even compete against other runners, only against themselves. Even among those who do compete, running is the only sport I know in which a person can come in 1000th and still feel like a winner. I do not believe that athletic activity without the overtones of the Greek games is in conflict with the Jewish tradition.

Maimonides, the twelfth century philosopher and physician known also as Rambam, agrees. He writes:

> A person should not eat until he has walked enough for his body to become flushed, or he should engage in some other task or strenuous activity. The general principle is that one should strain one's body every morning until it has become flushed, rest a little until breathing is returned to normal and then eat. (*Yad: Hilkhot Deyot,* 4:2.)

And

> Nothing is to be found that can substitute for exercise in any way....exercise will expel the harm done by most of the bad regimens that most men follow. Not all motion is exercise. Exercise is powerful or rapid motion or a

combination of both, vigorous motion which alters breathing and increases its rate. (*The Regimen of Health,* Chapter 1)

No one would be surprised to find such quotes in any of the current books on the virtues of exercise. But medieval philosophers generally believed that the best thing to do with the body was to get rid of it. When one of them expresses such convictions, then we had better pay careful attention. Rambam knew that his mind would work better if his body did.

Most of our mental images of this pious and great scholar would picture him deep in thought at his desk, hunched over his manuscripts with several volumes of the Talmud open on the table before him. I propose another image, not to replace this one, but to add to it. From time to time, we should also think of Maimonides panting down an Egyptian street, shortly before the dawn, wearing whatever might have been the twelfth century equivalent of a sweat suit, with the glow on his face that can only be gotten from a good run. Perhaps he is trying to solve a difficult philosophic problem or determine what to prescribe for one of his sick patients. His head is clear and soon he will be ready to return to the world of the intellect. He has rejected those aspects of the Greek world that need to be rejected and taken those that have merit. He doesn't feel any less Jewish because he is using his body.

The Piece Of Pork

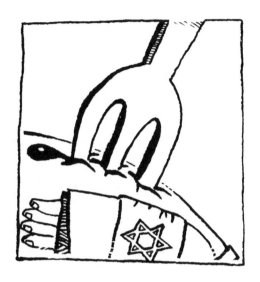

I had a piece of pork
and put it on a fork
and gave it to the curly
headed Jew, Jew, Jew.

his nineteenth-century ditty, used throughout the English speaking world, is one I had not known until I read about it. The curious thing about the rhyme is that though it makes no specifically derogatory references to

Jews, it is quite clearly anti-Semitic. As far as I can tell, it has dropped out of use. At least none of the children I know are familiar with it. But though the rhyme may have died, the theme it touches is live and well.

My greyhound Giggles and I, well known eccentrics of our neighborhood, have not missed a day of running for a long time. We regularly stop in for water and a bit of socializing at a firehouse that is about three miles from my house. Giggles usually seems to enjoy running five or six miles with me, but if she sees from the route that we are going to go out for ten or fifteen miles and the weather is especially bad or if she simply doesn't feel like running far on a particular day, she will turn around and trot home. Not a dumb dog, Giggles. Before going all the way home, she frequently stops and waits for me a while at the familiar firehouse to see if I will come back and get her, as I often do.

A few months ago, before going to the synagogue on a religious holiday, I ran a long loop that didn't much appeal to Giggles. When I realized that she had left me, I decided that I couldn't go back and pick her up and still get to services on time that morning. I kept right on going.

She did not return home as soon as usual. I didn't know where she was, but since she knows our town as well as I do, and she is not a wanderer, I was confident that she would turn up sooner or later.

During the day, the answering machine kept taking messages, but we didn't pay any attention to them until after dark at the end of the holiday. Then I learned that Giggles was still waiting at the firehouse and would I please come and pick her up right away.

Though the firemen know Giggles well and like her, when I got there, they made it clear that they were a little miffed that they had been stuck with her for the day. Nevertheless, they seemed more than adequately compensated by the pleasure they got from telling me how

"The Pork on the Fork: A Nineteenth Century Anti-Jewish Ditty," Jonathan D. Sarna, *Jewish Social Studies*, Spring 1982, Volume 44, pp. 169-172

much she enjoyed the half of a ham sandwich they fed her. I heard the story again when we stopped in the next day. By this time it was a huge piece of ham they had fed the rabbi's dog. By the third day, it was practically a whole suckling pig. Each time they retold the story in my presence to other men in the firehouse, both the piece of pork, and Giggles' gusto in eating it, had grown.

The mysterious and powerful connection between Jews and pork far transcends the technicalities of Jewish law. The Bible tells us that we don't eat pork because the pig is one of the animals that doesn't chew its cud. But eating it has come to mean much more than that. Eating shellfish or milk and meat together may not be very Jewish in a traditional sense, but eating pork is downright anti-Semitic.

For a Jew to eat lobster means that he does not accept the strictures of Jewish law. For a non-Jew to offer it, even to an observant Jew, is at worst a social gaffe. On the other hand, for a Jew to eat pork suggests either active self-hate or utter estrangement from the basic symbols of Jewish culture. For a non-Jew to offer a Jew (or in this case, even his dog) pork, is a gesture that can carry with it heavy anti-Semitic overtones.

Though I do not think my gruff, jovial firemen friends who are my daily hosts would knowingly hurt me, they were in possession of a set of associations that resonated quite deeply in their cultural experience, even though they probably could not have articulated clearly what they were. They only knew that "they had a piece of pork and put it on a fork etc., etc."

Hives and Blisters:
Some Unconventional Paths To Spiritual Discovery

I have always earned my living as a civil servant of the Jewish community. Most of my professional time has been taken up with writing letters and making phone calls, the bread and butter of bureaucratic life. I am for the most part a rather straight, conventional and not especially distinguished rabbi/administrator. To the extent that I am unconventional, my eccentricities do not extend much beyond the one hundred and fifty pounds of honey I try to get annually from my bee-hives and the one or two marathons I run every year. I used to drive around town on a motor-scooter, but I gave that up.

Along with the other members of a discussion group, I was recently asked to tell three things about myself, one of them a lie. Then, we were told to try to identify each other's lies. I said that I was a runner, a beekeeper and an administrator. My lie was that I was an administrator. Even though I spend many hours performing administrative tasks, I do not view myself as an administrator in any important way. I may be deceiving myself to protect my own self image, just as David Ben-Gurion, Israel's first Prime Minister, listed his occupation on his identity card as "farmer," but it is the posture I find most congenial. I view administration like chess; it is an interesting game; Sometimes you lose, sometimes you win. But my inner spirit is not bound up with the activity.

The questions I was asked in the discussion group led to my reflections on the three essentially unrelated forces that do seem to energize my life: Judaism, which gives me structure; beekeeping which gives me focus; and running, which brings a sense of joy, optimism and perspective to my basically cynical and suspicious nature.

My Jewishness locates me in time as part of an ancient tradition. It demands that I reflect upon the changes of the seasons and the passing of the years. My Jewishness makes me consider my relationship to my people, to other peoples. It ties me to a series of issues and behaviors—and I need to be anchored.

Beekeeping is my tool for centering. Bees are fierce Zen masters. They demand total concentration. If given complete attention, they are gentle, harmless and productive. On a nice day I can tend my hives wearing only a pair of running shorts and running sneakers. No protective nets, no gloves, and not even a shirt. But if my thoughts wander, even for a moment, the bees serve me notice and I am quickly punished. I mustn't move rapidly or make jerky motions. I must be careful not to crush them. I have got to use enough smoke, but not too much smoke. I must be sure the weather is just right and that the flowers from which they have been gathering are open. If I am not completely present to my bees, I will have cause for regret.

Once, I foolishly opened a hive shortly after a rainstorm. When they can't earn a living, bees become very irritable. Within thirty seconds, I had sixty stings on each ankle. Now I pay better attention. After a half an hour of well centered work with my hives, my mind is extraordinarily refreshed. They give me a kind of directedness of thought that I would find difficult to attain without them.

But if I need to be tied down, and need to be forced to direct my thoughts, I also need to be free, to let myself go. I have to be able to explore my inner self and the world around me. And that is why I am a runner.

Jungian writers, interested in the great legends, often describe what they believe to be the all-inclusive hero story, the mono-myth. In one version, the central figure goes off into the wilderness to prepare himself for the monumental task. Once readied, he goes in search of The Holy. His search leads him into a perilous land where he encounters great dangers. He is helped by a sage or wizard to overcome these hazards. The sage provides little, but what he does provide is essential to the hero's success.

The hero achieves his goal and often wins a beautiful maiden in the process. It is wonderful on the mountain, in the castle, at the burning bush or in Nirvana. He is sorely tempted to remain in the world of his quest where he has achieved perfect wisdom and understanding, but he inevitably chooses to return to tell the tale.

around with the patience to organize fifty mile races, the only one who will stay with the runners no matter how long it takes them to finish and no matter what the weather.

"Fred, I can't do it," I gasp. "I am quitting."

"You are doing nothing of the sort, young man. Get out there and walk a few laps. You don't look like much, but you'll be just fine. Next year you ought to train before you try one of these things. I didn't sit out here in the rain for all these hours counting the times you went around for you to quit in the middle. It's all in your head, young feller. I am telling you that you are in much better shape than you think. You can do it. Here, have some of my super sweet tea. That will pick you up."

He is a good wizard. A little guilt, a little expertise, some mild chastening, a few words of encouragement, some magic brew and off I go. Each of the three times I tried to stop, Fred drove me out again.

By the thirty-fifth mile, the worst is over. I know I can always walk the last fifteen miles if I have to. I begin to count backwards towards the diminishing number of miles left rather than adding up the miles already run. I still ache just as much as I did at thirty miles, but I have come to terms with the hurt. I no longer fight it. My body is no longer very important. I have somehow transcended pain.

Nevertheless, I am extraordinarily sensitive to being touched. Someone gives me an encouraging pat as I go by. It enrages me. A physician friend who works in the medical aid station at the end of the Boston Marathon told me that their medical team tries hard not to touch stressed runners, who frequently flail out. Even enthusiastic friends and family who hug a finishing runner will sometimes get pushed or punched. I had read about Tibetan monks who train for one hundred mile runs by meditating in holes in the ground. They are said to run at incredible speeds, but if touched, they die. Though it sounds a little crazy, right now it makes sense to me.

Something odd was also happening to George, another runner, who had been keeping about the same pace I was. It had rained earlier in the day and there were still a lot of puddles around. Instead of running the straightest route he could, George kept zig-zagging from puddle to puddle and running through them. I asked him why he was splashing his way along, rather than running as best he could like the rest of us. He smiled a silly smile and said, "I have very broad feet. Quack. Quack. Quack." So I was now a Tibetan monk and George had turned into a duck. I wondered whom everyone else had become.

In the last five miles, my speed picked up amazingly. My son Joshua, who was fifteen at the time, had been accompanying me these last miles. He is a pretty good runner, but was starting to have trouble keeping up. I suddenly realized that Fred was right. The hurt was far more in my head than my feet. I must never again give myself excuses about what I can and can't do. If I want something enough, there are many fewer things that stand in my way than I would dearly love to claim.

At the fiftieth mile, I was very pleased. Far too tired for elation. I was just quietly satisfied. I had done something very hard. I didn't quit. I never have and never will come in first, but I have never quit either. Joshua asked me why I did it. I said I didn't know. He was insistent. "To run fifty miles, you *must* know."

By the next day, when the real high came, I had begun to get some glimmerings. Though I was stiff that morning, I was less stiff than I had anticipated. I ran, but not very fast or very far. Though running has done wonderful things for my cardiovascular system, it hasn't done very much at all for my feet. They were still revoltingly and painfully blistered. But none of it mattered because the world seemed whole.

I had a much clearer sense of who I was, and what is and what is not important in the world. I have no illusions that my race was of any real significance, but whatever it is in the human psyche that makes people go off on perilous journeys in order to come back with new perceptions of the world, I too have shared. It may be only endorphins or chemicals producing an effect analogous to that of LSD or mountain climbing, but that doesn't matter to me. The experience was too powerful a force to trivialize.

It is not the classic Jewish way to spirituality. I personally must remain seriously attached to the traditional Jewish patterns lest I become too self-indulgent about my private revelations, but I am grateful for what I have been able to discover through my own adventures. I am returned to tell the tale. With Job, I can say, "From out of my flesh, I shall see God" (Job 19:27).

Epilogue

You Can't Do it All on One Foot

 few months ago, driving cross-town in a Manhattan taxi, my Korean cab driver turned far enough around to start a conversation and asked, "Where are you from?" "Boston," I said.

Then, since that answer was apparently not sufficiently rewarding, clearly not what he was after, he asked, "And what are your origins?"

What *are* my origins?...I thought to myself. Chicago is where I was born but could I call Chicago my *origins*? What about England, where my father's family comes from? But who knows how long they were there? Eastern Europe, the birthplace of my mother's family? But if we are talking about origins, maybe I should opt for Asia Minor and Palestine? Mt. Sinai? Ur, Abraham's home town? While I was trying to unravel the meaning of the question, and simultaneously formulate an answer which was at once accurate and intelligible, the driver turned again.

"You are taking too long to answer," he said. "You must be Jewish."

That driver had immediately penetrated to the core of the Jewish experience. There is very little that is straight-forward; few matters that can be summarized in clear, crisp statements, the functional equivalent of "I'm from Korea."

Since that incident, whenever I hear myself launching into an involved response to one of those interesting question that give me so much delight, I can hear him whispering into my ear, "You are taking too long. You must be Jewish." But then, in my head I answer him, "Who said it had to be quick and simple?"

Perhaps I have been unreasonably indirect. Though the essays in this book may seem to be somewhat frivolous in style, I have intended throughout that they should deal with real issues. Even though I am at the end of this book, it may be worthwhile to recount something of the context out of which both I and the ideology of the book emerge.

I come from a Reform Jewish background, the most liberal wing of the Jewish religious tradition. Our family was not doctrinaire, deeply committed or especially knowledgeable Reform; rather, we were normative, mostly passive, but not indifferent. We were certainly more than High Holy Day attending Reform Jews. I went to Sunday school from kindergarten through post-Confirmation and even high school and liked it very much. My home synagogue was one of the last holdouts of radical Reform Judaism. Major services were only held on Sunday mornings. Jewish holidays were not observed on the dates they fell according to the Jewish calendar, but instead, on the nearest Sunday.

It was within my memory that a major decision had to be made when the synagogue Cub Scout Troop wanted to hold religious services on a Friday night, the evening most Jews throughout the world begin the celebration of the Shabbat. The board of directors met in solemn assembly to determine whether the Shabbat now comes on Sundays, the day that most Jews are free to observe a day of rest, or if it still comes on Friday night, despite the difficulties of observing the Shabbat at that time. All credit to the board, in spite of the religiously radical traditions of that synagogue, they determined that the Cub Scouts could hold the service since the Shabbat still falls on Friday night and Saturday but the congregation would continue to hold services on Sunday, even though it was a mere weekday in the Jewish calendar. As a result of the pioneering spirit of those Cub Scouts, a modest Friday evening service is now held in addition to the big Sunday morning service. There is little that this synagogue represents that today I could call my own, but then I liked it well enough and I am more than grateful to it for that.

Our family regularly celebrated holidays, though hardly in what could be called traditional fashion. Bread was not served during Passover, but there was no reason to remove the bacon from the house. We celebrated Hanukkah, faithfully lighting the candles, but we gave presents for Christmas and even had a tree for a few years. Though perhaps not typical today, this pattern did not seem very peculiar then. As a matter of fact, it was the way most of our friends comported themselves. At that time, it was part of the balance that seemed appropriate to the way we defined ourselves as Jews and Americans. What is shared by a community has a way of seeming reasonable, no matter how outlandish it is in fact, a realization which makes me a little nervous to this day.

Throughout my growing up, Judaism seemed reasonably interesting. More accurately, some of the people who seemed to care about Judaism seemed interesting, but clearly the substance of the tradition was neither clear nor important. Judaism was worth bothering about, but not bothering about very much.

Not too long ago, a young man who grew up in a synagogue like mine, told me that his rabbi so convinced him that everything in Judaism was in complete accord with the best in modern thought, that he felt it made perfect sense to abandon Judaism and stick to modern thought. To him it seemed much cleaner that way. If you accept the original premise, as many of my peers at that time would have, he was probably right.

As I was about to go off to college, I had vague notions about wanting to write, or teach English, or maybe do some sort of social work. Since none of our family members had yet recovered from their business failures of the great depression, I had no clear career aspirations, other than knowing that I didn't want to go into business. It was during this period of late high-school that all of the adult males on my father's side of the family changed their names from Israel to vaguely Anglo-Saxon appellations.

The argument was that this had nothing to do with self-hate, but was only a simple practical measure. It had been hard enough to make a living during the depression, and there were a lot of people who didn't like Jews. In retrospect, it looks very odd. These brothers were in the millinery business all of their lives. They had the same business connections after they changed their names that they had beforehand and since most everyone in the business those days was Jewish anyway, it is not clear to me to whom they were trying to appear as non-Jews.

Nevertheless, they all agreed that if I wanted to be a successful writer some day, that I would have to have the right kind of name. Malamud, Roth and Bellow hadn't made it yet. The future was said to be bleak for those who could be publicly identified as Jews. Was it because of their urging or because of my own inner fears about being a Jew? I'll never know. Choosing between the two going names our family liked, Isbell and Cordell, I chose Cordell and kept it for about a year.

At the University of Chicago, where the next part of the story takes place, my initial "Jewish" crisis came in the first week of school. Placement exams were to be held on the first day of Rosh ha-Shanah, the Jewish New Year. What was I to do? I had always gone to services on the holidays. I wish I could say that I struggled long and hard over the question but it only took me about thirty seconds to decide that I was not going to let anything as trivial as a Jewish holiday disrupt my academic career. I was certainly going to take the exam as scheduled. Having made up my mind, I went to sign up. It was then that I saw the notice that was posted. All Jewish students could take a substitute exam a few days later with no penalty. I was rather ashamed. I had been willing to sell out and it was not even necessary.

Some two weeks later, for reasons I no longer remember, I wandered into the university's Hillel Foundation, the center for Jewish student activity. A service was going on, a service which was very different from the almost all English service I knew from my own synagogue. It was very distasteful to me: The murmuring sounds, the bobbing heads, the strange language...none of this was mine. Two impulses became clear to me simultaneously; that I wanted out and that I didn't know enough to walk out legitimately. It was only much later I learned that mine was a good Jewish response. An *apikorus*, a knowledgeable atheist who rejects the tradition, gets a kind of grudging respect in Judaism. A mere ignoramus gets none.

In any event, I became actively involved in the life of the Hillel Foundation, for it was the only place where I had hope of discovering the solutions to my various spiritual and identity questions. Upon pursuing Judaism seriously for the first time, I was amazed at how excitingly promising the literature was. Though it sounds rather dumb to say it, I discovered, for example, that the Bible was really a pretty good book after all and I was surprised and delighted.

Within months, the direction in which I was going was clear enough that I felt I wanted to and had earned the right to reclaim the name Israel as my own; after all, it was the name Jacob was given after he had wrestled with God. This thrust remained sufficiently consistent that a few years later when I still had no clear notion of what I wanted to do in this world, continuing my Jewish education at a rabbinical seminary seemed to be a perfectly appropriate thing to do. Be a rabbi? Ridiculous! But a seminary would be a splendid place for a person who was an intellectual dilettante to continue his studies and his searchings, especially since it didn't cost much. Off I went to the Reform rabbinical school, the Hebrew Union College-Jewish Institute of Religion in Cincinnati.

It was early in my career that I discovered that a rabbinic school, or at least that one, was *not* designed to solve spiritual problems. During the spring of my first year the freshman students were assigned the task of developing a special afternoon worship service and barbecue. Since in the time of the ancient Temple in Jerusalem roast lamb, among other things, was offered up at the afternoon service, the notion of a service and barbecue made a bizzare kind of sense. We were an eager lot and so we decided to add some creative prayers to the otherwise rote service. The group of us was gathered in someone's small dormitory room. Things were not going well. The hour for the service was approaching. We were getting tense; it was our rabbinic "coming out" party and we weren't ready. A few of the fellows began to work off their tensions by clowning around. Another student barked at them..."Cut it out, will you! Let's get the goddamn prayers written already."

It was an important moment of truth. At that instant, I definitively discovered that I was not in a place of Torah, but rather in a rather sophisticated trade school. I was not embittered by this discovery. In fact, it gave me a better perspective into what I had a right to expect. This brief experience liberated me from the system and freed me to develop on my own those personal, intellectual and spiritual relationships which might help me grow. I learned then what the Midrash, that classic collection of rabbinic homilies, had pointed out years earlier—that it was not by accident that God revealed the Torah in the desert. Unless you are thirsty, you don't seek out the living waters of Torah.

Believing that I was located in a spiritual desert, I concluded that I could nevertheless gain a great deal on a one-to-one basic from fellow students and faculty members. Some of both were dull careerists but there were many others who were exciting and wise and who nourished me generously.

None of the rabbinic schools knows precisely what its goals are or how to achieve even the conflicting goals they have. They know that teaching Torah alone will not prepare someone to be a rabbi, but neither will teaching a trade, the rabbinic trade, suffice. And so they vacillate and do their best to muddle through. Though I hated the school while there, at this point I have nothing but compassion for those who attempt to run such an enterprise. They still do it badly, but I don't know how I would do it any better.

After some four years of considerable effort to acquire an elementary Jewish education (I was not very good at Hebrew), I was still determined to become Jewishly knowledgeable. I decided that if I wanted to become a Jew, Israel was probably a more promising place to study than Cincinnati. After a short period of studying at the Hebrew University, I concluded that it offered me little more than the same materials I had been getting in Cincinnati, only in Hebrew. Having gone to all the trouble of going to Israel, I felt that I should at least get something that I did not have access to back home, so off I went to a kibbutz yeshivah, an old fashioned rabbinic academy, but one that was located on a collective settlement. It was a good experience. I did not have a blinding conversion. In many respects, I was quite resistant to much that the yeshivah had to offer, but I did settle one major intellectual problem, the kind of Jew I was going to be.

The omnipresence of arms tattooed with concentration camp numbers was a grim continuing reminder of the murder of six million of my people and convincing evidence that our history should have come to an end. Yet there to testify to our continued vitality was the incredible existence of a Jewish state in the modern world. The absurd fact of my existence as a Jew became the starting point of my personal credo. Personal religious experience led me only to general religious concern, not to Judaism. Reason and history only told me why I should not exist. I came to take my unlikely presence in the world today as a Jew to be more than a mere biological or sociological fact. A positivist cannot explain me without standing on his head. Given its character and quality, it was impossible for me to conceptualize the Jewish experience without ascribing to it a teleology.

There are two midrashim, rabbinic homilies, which describe that formative event in Jewish history known as the giving of the Torah. One tells of the people of Israel standing at the foot of Mt. Sinai while God tells them either to take the Torah or expect that the mountain will be turned over and cover them. Mt. Sinai would become their burial place. The second tells of God in effect peddling the Torah from people to people until Israel finally accepts it freely and enthusiastically.

The first midrash describes my willy-nilly chosenness; the fact that my parents were Jews and didn't ask me if I wanted to be born that way any more than did their parents or their parents' parents right back to Sinai. How I respond to the fact of my Jewishness seems to be described by the second midrash. In it, I am not chosen, I choose. So my options are either to choose willingly to accept the Torah or to try to escape from it. I have inherited an estate. Whether I choose to live in it is for me to determine.

I did not find the idea of chosenness to be a self-aggrandizing embarrassment. I took it to mean that the Jew still has a role to play in God's plan for the resolution of history. I see no great intellectual scandal in assuming that God wants to work out history through particular peoples as opposed to all of humanity together. One makes as much or as little sense as the other and my personal experience drew me to conclude the former set of assumptions worked best for me.

The event at Sinai placed me here today. Even though the precise nature of that event is not clear from the texts, I believe that the Torah is the record of the response to whatever it was that happened. What is clear is that that happening had an irrevocable impact upon a people for several thousand years. I, as a member of that people, am affected by and thus ultimately a participant in the event. If the acceptance of the commandments was the response of the people in that time to Sinai, insofar as I wished to participate in and personally recover that moment in history, I had to participate in the commandments.

But insofar as there is a lack of clarity about the event, there is also a lack of clarity about the commandments. I could accept the idea of the law and its general structure. I was not certain about the authority of its particulars. There was a revelation but its full content was not always obvious. There were commandments, but I had to struggle to discover them.

For a long time, I had been troubled by the Jewish religious liberal's eternal question: What is the true spirit of Judaism? What is really the essential quality of the tradition? Is it justice? Ethics? Piety? Jewish peoplehood? When all was said and done, I came to a conclusion that brings no great shock to Jewish traditionalists.

We have had many internal squabbles in the course of Jewish history. The prophets fought with the priests, the Pharisees with the Sadducees, the followers of the rabbinic tradition fought with the biblicist position of the Karaites, the Hasidim had their opponents. These groups disagreed with each other on some very basic issues. They argued about which was the right law and who gets to make decisions about it, but one issue never seriously came into question: whether Jewish law was itself essential. Thus it seemed to me that if I wanted to play the Jewish religious game, the only way it could be played legitimately included paying serious attention to the niceties of *halakhah*, Jewish law. I decided that I wanted to play the game.

I didn't especially like these conclusions. It was quite inconvenient but I saw no way to escape it. I felt quite self-conscious about practicing observances which were in no way a customary part of my life. I felt particularly foolish about my observance later on in the presence of my non-observant professors at rabbinic school. My conduct felt like an implicit judgment on their way of life. I knew perfectly well that they were far more learned than I was ever likely to become, that most of them had come via the route I was now taking and had abandoned it long since. I was certain they had no idea about what I was really undertaking and I clearly appeared to all the world like an ignorant fanatic, a type I personally despise.

I did not accommodate myself to the rigors of Jewish law because they were divinely ordained, or because they were beautiful and meaningful, but only because if I wished to be a religious Jew there was no other way to do it with authenticity and honesty to the tradition. The question of the divinity of the law would just have to wait.

Though I did not feel free to ignore consideration of any of them, the mitzvot (the traditional commandments), affected me variously. Some, whether in the ethical or ritual realm felt like rare opportunities, to be passed by only at my deep personal loss. Rabbi Mendel of Kotzk once said, "I don't want you to sin, not because it is wrong, but because there isn't enough time." I cannot say that the important issue in the non-observance of the Shabbat is a sin, but it certainly is a missed opportunity which can never be recovered. A Shabbat that I have missed can never happen to me again. I have lost it.

I do not feel the same about all of the commandments. Some are deeply enriching, some are bothersome and still others are silent. But my negative or indifferent response to a commandment does not necessarily provide me with an immediate and automatic release. It would be easy for me to rearrange and reinterpret until the entire corpus is up-to-date, but if history teaches me anything, it teaches that today's fads are not necessarily tomorrow's faith. God may be dead this week, living in mushrooms next and the following week merely a figure of speech for Another, who is really God. My own religious temperament required a certain amount of rootedness. I was prepared to live in contact with the regulations of the tradition so that they might teach me, while I suspended judgment about their metaphysical validity.

I do not want to cut myself off from the possibility of being judged by the tradition. If I casually drop bothersome aspects of it, I will never again have the opportunity to be challenged by its difficult ideas, nor will I give the generations that come after me the opportunity to recover a meaning which I have lost. I am involved in a religious holding operation.

If I had dropped commandments which were annoying, I certainly would have dropped the Jewish dietary laws, whose provocative quality is one of its chief virtues for my religious life, keeping me religiously aware when it would be much simpler just to eat when hungry.

I also feel myself under pressure to push myself forward to explore new material, to try to observe one more commandment today than I did yesterday, though sometimes I slip backwards and without much guilt.

I do not find it possible to observe or confront all of the commandments which my tradition hands me. Some are much more do-able than others. Some are more comfortable than others. If it really makes me miserable, I stand back from it. Though I believe in a certain amount of religious discomfort, I am not committed to hair-shirt religion. If a religion makes someone feel terrible all of the time, there is something wrong with the religion, or at least with the fit. I would add to that something that the Dali Lama was recently quoted as saying, that if it doesn't make people kinder to one another, it probably isn't religion.

At this time of my life I feel more comfortable being a Jew than I was when I first jumped in. I no longer want to be more or better during my every waking moment. I am more relaxed with where I am, no longer searching continually for major new truths or powerful teachers. I no longer want to push every idea to its logical conclusion. In fact, I have come to believe that any good idea pushed to its logical conclusion is probably wrong. I want to learn new ideas and new facts but am not actively seeking new basic insights with which to restructure my life. As someone who was once a rather intense truth seeker, this is a somewhat new phenomenon for me, but I assume that it is probably age-related and therefore endurable.

As one who is, I think, not atypical of these times, I find it requires a considerable act of will to take the Jewish categories seriously. It is much simpler to live cozily with the twentieth century liberal, pragmatic, empiricist tradition into which I was born. But I was born into two worlds and there is more to my life as a Jew than today's intellectual climate alone can sustain. Jewish law at least offers me an opportunity to be in continuing contact with the categories of the Jewish tradition that I may come to grips with them in their own terms. What I find is that Jewish law makes me ask some very good questions and that is always better than getting very good answers.

When the time came to leave Egypt and Pharaoh wanted to know what the people of Israel would do once they left, Moses said to Pharaoh, *"We will not know in what way we will serve the Lord until we get there."* (Exodus. 10:3)

That statement says a good deal about the Jewish religious search. What we will find is not altogether clear, but we do have an obligation to go and endure the demands of the trip. And if whatever we learn along the way does not lend itself to snappy answers, so much the worse for the questioners. From time to time, we may have to deliver on some of the basics when standing on one foot or sitting in a cross-town cab. But the really interesting things, which are far more complicated, may yet be out there waiting to be discovered by those prepared to engage in continuing conversation with our past. And what better way is there to contribute to the conversation than with some good stories?

NOTES

"The Kosher Pig, When Jewish Law Doesn't Quite Work." Originally published in *Moment*, 7:3 (March 1982).

"Torah and Telephones." Originally published as part of "Meditations About The Art of Sympathy" *The Melton Journal*, 18 (Summer 1984), p. 13.

"On Baldness and the Jewish Problem." Originally published in *Moment*, 9:1 (December 1983), p. 9.

"How to Survive your Synagogue." Originally published in *The Second Jewish Catalog*, Jewish Publication Society, 1976.

"How to Give a D'var Torah: A Beginner's Guide." Originally published in *New Traditions, Explorations in Judaism*, 2 (Spring 1985), National Havurah Committee, pp. 90-103.

"Speed *Davening*." originally published as "What's Your Hurry, Amen. The Curious Phenomenon of Speed *Davening*." *Moment*, 10:8 (September 1985).

"Hospitality Should be Practiced Religiously." Originally published as "Hakhnasat Orḥim/ Hospitality." in *The Jewish Catalog*, Jewish Publication Society, 1973

"The Late Jewish People." Originally published in *Moment*, 10: 3 (March 1985).

"Fast Food." originally published as "Fast Advice." *Hadassah Magazine*, 65:1 (August/September 1983).

"Jewish Haute Cuisine." Originally published in *Hadassah Magazine*, 66:5 (January 1985).

"Why Jewish Wine Tastes Terrible." Originally published in *Moment*, 11:4 (April 1986).

"Memorable Weddings." Originally published as "Rites (and Wrongs) of Spring: Memorable Weddings I Have Known." *Moment*, 10:6 (June 1985).

"Washing the Dead." originally published as "My Friend Gorelick & The Angel of Death." *Moment*, 9:8 (September 1984).

"The Spurious Kaddish." Originally published in *Moment*, 9:10 (November 1984),

"Judaism and Jogging, or: The Rambam Wore Sweats." Originally published in *Moment*, 4:5 (May 1979).

"The Piece of Pork." Originally published in *The Baltimore Jewish Times*, 166:1 (January 3, 1986).

"Hives and Blisters." Originally published as "Bee Hives and Blisters: Some Unconventional Paths to Spiritual Discovery." *Moment*, 7:9 (October 1982).

"Bee-ing and Being." Originally published in different form as "The Promised Land of Milk and Date Jam—The Problems of Bee-ing in the Bible and the Talmud." *B'nai Brith The International Jewish Monthly*, 87:3 (November 1972), B'nai B'rith International.

"Jews and Wasps: Cultures in Conflict." Originally published as "Jews and Wasps: Cultures in Conflict or The Unwelcome Guests of Sukkot." *The Baltimore Jewish Times*, 170:7, (October 17, 1986).

"Epilogue." Includes material originally published as "On Being and Becoming a Rabbi." *Dimensions*, 5:1 (Fall 1970) published by the Union of American Hebrew Congregations, and also from untitled essay in "The Condition of Jewish Belief: A Symposium." *Commentary*, 42:2 (August 1966).

Temple Israel

Minneapolis, Minnesota

IN HONOR OF
THE BAR MITZVAH OF
JOEL REISS
FROM
SIDNEY & MARILYN WEISBERG